Shettleston Library
154 Wellshot Road
Glasgow G32 7AX
Phone: 0141 276 1643 Fax 276 1645

This book is due for return on or before the last date shown below. It may be renewed by telephone, personal application, fax or post, quoting this date, author, title and the book number

- 2 SEP 2015

Glasgow Life and its service brands, including Glasgow Libraries, (found at www.glasgowlife.org.uk) are operating names for Culture and Sport Glasgow

THE LOVE OF AN
UNKNOWN SOLDIER

THE LOVE OF AN UNKNOWN SOLDIER

LOVE LETTERS FOUND IN A TRENCH

UNIFORM
PRESS

Uniform Press Ltd
66 Charlotte Street
London
W1T 4QE

www.uniformpress.co.uk

First published in 1918 by John Lane
This edition published in 2015 by Uniform Press Ltd

978-1-910065-45-7

5 4 3 2 1

Printed in India by Imprint Digital
Designed by Charlotte Glyde

PUBLISHER'S FOREWORD
1918

The publication of documents as intimate as those printed in this little volume requires some explanation and apology, but I venture to think that my reasons will be found sufficient.

The MS. was submitted to me by a young officer of the R.F.A., home from the front on leave, who had just read 'The MS in a Red Box.' This circumstance, he admitted, had decided him to consult me. He explained that he had brought with him from France a bundle of papers which he had found in one of the dug-outs of an abandoned gun position. To use his own words: 'The position was in a hell of a mess.' It had been badly knocked about by enemy bombardments, and had obviously been rendered untenable.

He discovered the papers secreted in a dark corner, wedged in between a post and the wall of one of the bunks. At first he thought they might be papers of military importance, for the care with which they had been hidden showed that they had been considered valuable. This fact alone aroused his curiosity. When he had time to examine them carefully, he discovered that he was prying into the intimate secret of a brother officer, who was in all probability dead. There was no indication of the writer's name or of his unit, and the name of the girl whom he had loved was never recorded, so the people most intimately concerned were left entirely anonymous. His first impulse was to respect the dead man's privacy and destroy the papers, but on second thoughts he recognized that they were the sacred property of the woman who had inspired such adoration and courage.

On thinking the matter over, he began to feel more and more strongly that they ought to be given back to that woman, but the difficulty of doing so seemed insuperable. Many divisions had been in that area, and it would be impossible to trace the batteries of the various brigades which had occupied those gun pits. It was under these circumstances that he told me the story, hoping that the mystery surrounding these letters might in some such way be solved as the unknown author of 'The MS in a Red Box' was eventually discovered. On reading the tattered MS., I was from the first impressed with its literary value; but as I read on I became more and more deeply absorbed in its poignant human importance, especially in its importance to some particular American girl, who, all unknowingly, had quickened the last days of this unknown soldier's life with romance. I felt that she must be discovered, and that the only chance of doing so was by publishing the documents.

Somewhere in France, where she is carrying on her work of mercy, this little book may stray into her hands. If it does, she will certainly recognize herself, and remember those days of kindness which meant so much to a young English officer, on leave in Paris. Should this happen, I want her to know that the original papers, which were meant for her only and rescued by chance from a crumbling dug-out, are awaiting her in my office, and will be handed over as soon as she presents herself.

Meanwhile, I ask her pardon for this necessary means of making known to the world the romance that she kindled in the heart of her lost soldier, which he himself did not tell her.

THE LOVE OF AN
UNKNOWN SOLDIER

I

SO it is all over. It was only a dream which happened in my brain. We have said goodbye, and I have not told you. I was so many times on the point of telling you – every evening after I had left you I accused myself and spent half the night awake planning the words in which I would confess when next we met. But we have come to our last night and I have kept silent; tomorrow I return to the Front, leaving you almost as much a stranger as when we met.

I wonder if you have guessed. Surely I could not have loved you so much without your knowing. And yet – yes, I am glad that I said nothing. What right have I, who may be dead within a month, to speak to you of love? To have done so would have been the act of a coward.

I want to put the case to myself so that I may act strongly. If I had spoken and you had loved me in return, what would have resulted? Only suffering – until the war is ended, we could never have been together – and you, all the time you would have been lonely. All the time you would have been worrying about my safety. If I were wounded again, you would think me dead. Though I were badly wounded, you would not be able to come to me, for you, too, have your duty up there behind the Front at J————, you and the other American girls who take care of the French babies. And then I might have been maimed. With the French a man's wounds are like decorations, they are tokens of the new religion – of sacrifice. With us they are still horrible. I would not have you held to your bargain with a maimed man, for I might have to live to see you shudder. And, then, I may die in this war – who can tell? If I had married you, I should have stolen your happiness and left you deserted. No, I am glad I did not speak of love.

But why talk? If I had, you would probably have looked offended and have refused me – refused me as I deserved. You would have acted rightly, for I don't believe in these war-engagements and war-marriages. Still – the heart cries out; it is difficult to say "No" to self when one is young. I will not think of these things; they make me distracted.

And yet there is still time to tell you. I have only to unhook the receiver and to telephone to you. If I did, what would you say? A queer way to receive a proposal! At past midnight to be roused from sleep to hear a spectral voice saying, "Is that Miss ————? This is the man who's been with you all the evening – almost every evening, in fact, of his leave in Paris. I called you up to ask if you'd marry me?"

I won't think of might-have-beens, but only of the

12

memories. They'll be good memories to run over when one's cold and wet and cheerless in some caved-in trench. I shall tell myself the fairy story then of how I met you, how I pledged myself to meet you again, and by accident kept my word.

Do you remember that night, some months ago, when I had been wounded, and had been sent to America on the British Mission? It was soon after America had become our Ally, and I was speaking on the splendour of men's souls in the trenches. At the close, when the hall was emptying, some one brought you up and introduced us. They said that you were sailing for France with a unit that was going to take care of little children in the devastated districts. I looked into your eyes. What did I see there? Something haunting that I never shall forget. There you stood – a tall, slim girl, like a rosebud on a stem with its petals unfolding. I know devastated districts – I have helped to do the devastating. There are dead men mouldering in every shell-hole. I couldn't see you in that picture, you with your delicate fashionable sweetness. I don't know what I said. Can't remember. Something inadequately trivial about French children being dirty. We shook hands perfunctorily and parted. I sat up most of that night thinking. Next day I telephoned you to wish you luck, but really to hear your voice. You had already sailed. It was then that I pledged myself somehow to find you when I returned to France. How that was to be done I could not guess. I told myself it must happen – and it has.

Was it fate? Up there in the mud I was offered a leave to Paris long before my turn, chiefly because the other officers preferred to wait for Blighty leave and a good many of those who were ahead of me were dead. I came to Paris thinking, 'There's just a chance that I may see her.' I went to call on the only girl I knew and found you staying with her. Perhaps it was fate; I prefer to think that it was something else.

That first day I did not see you, but the next you called me up. I took it as an omen of good fortune that you should have gone to that trouble; it seemed to prove to me that to you also that hurried introduction had been more than an incident; that you, too, had been intrigued and made a trifle curious. My vanity, perhaps! But it was more than vanity. A man lives long dreams at the Front – all the best of the past and the tenderest of the insecure future; it is his way of compensating himself for the brevity of the life that he has.

It was a Sunday that we met. I had been so bold as to ask you to come to lunch, and you, quite wonderfully, had accepted. I think I remember every step and emotion of that walk up to the Champs-Elysées to call for you. You'd never guess how long I spent in polishing my belt and buttons. Yes, men are like that. Are you smiling? Perhaps you had spent just as long in making yourself beautiful. I should like to think that.

And my emotions! Shall I be frank? They were awfully muddled. They were made up of longing, hope, doubt and the terror that I might appear absurd. The longing was all for you. The hope was that you might be sharing my longing. The doubt was lest I might have idealized a memory which, when I saw you, would fade into reality. Oh, the heresy of me! I feared lest you might be actually quite ordinary, like any other of the many girls who crowd the world. And then my terror lest I

14

might appear absurd – I wonder if girls know it. You see, a man in love is at such a disadvantage; he is not sure that he is cared for in return. I had no right to that assurance – I, a mere stranger who had met you once.

I came to your hotel. When I inquired for you of the concierge, he seemed to distrust me. He answered me gruffly that he would apprise you of my presence. When he returned he informed me with jealous reluctance that Mademoiselle would presently descend. I waited. Heavens, how long I waited! It was five minutes probably; but it seemed a century. As each second ticked by I grew more and more dissatisfied with my conduct. How impertinent you must think me to presume on this slight acquaintance!

Your footstep on the stairs! A gentle rustling! You were standing before me, girlish and friendly, offering me the frailness of your hand. As I touched it a novel happiness swam through me. I felt alive, exalted and somehow rested – the way one does in hospital when one reckons up the days of one's probable respite from cold and fighting and discomfort. What I write is inadequate. It doesn't express a tithe of what I felt. I have spoken of the touch of your hand, but I think it was the sympathy in your eyes that touched me.

We were out in the Avenue, all shyness gone, the frost in the wind tingling against our faces. We caught a tram and lost ourselves; caught another and recognized where we were going. All the while we were chatting, asking questions and breaking in with new questions on each other's answers. Then we alighted and walked for the mere fun of walking. I suppose you'll never

15

know how proud I was to be seen beside you. You didn't notice how people paused to gaze after you. You wouldn't; one of your dearest qualities is your gay unconsciousness of self. But picture me, fresh from the defilement of battle-fields, where man's only hope is to die as heroically as he can; where one never sees a woman or children; where one dare not encourage tenderness lest one should become a coward; where all beauty, save of the soul, and every ambition for the future is blotted out. Here was I, a Lazarus restored from the dead, walking beside the most beautiful girl in Paris. It was wonderful, don't you think, to a man who had been so long buried that the earth was as yet scarcely out of his eyes?

The fun we had at the café where we went for lunch – do you remember that? The choosing of the courses! The way you concealed your smile at my halting French and at last came to my rescue! Our laughter at the curious people – all of them kind, but not all of them respectable! And who were we that we should laugh at others – we two who, by such strange chances, had found each other from all across the world?

When we left it was snowing, not hard but in little puffy flakes like jewels that settled on your hair and furs. I didn't want to lose you, so proposed a visit to the Luxembourg. By luck we found a taxi and, when the doors were shut, were for the first time alone together. It was a strange sensation. Our words faltered; we fell into a trembling silence. This aloneness, which I feared, was the thing which for months I had most desired. I felt so keenly aware of you; your beauty was almost painful. I wondered then, as I have wondered so many times, whether you had guessed. I can see you now – the clear profile of your face against the snow-covered window and the quiet tranquillity of your folded hands. You seemed unobtainable at that moment – a vision that would fade. My brain talked within itself, whispering things that were so true that they would have sounded ridiculous if uttered. And yet there was so little time. When one has counted one's life in seconds, one loses respect for the decorous divisions of weeks and months. I thought that with luck we might even be married before my leave, should end.

When once we were in public again our thoughts raced; we lost all fear of each other. There was one picture in the galleries that we stood before for a very long time: a fire-lit nursery table with a candle in the centre, children around it and a kind grey moon looking in at the window. It gave a touch of home and remembrance. The picture was by a Scotch artist who had visited me in my Oxford days; I told you how I had stolen a spray of chestnut once for the background to one of his pictures, breaking into the Warden's garden early one morning to do it.

We wandered out into the Gardens of the Luxembourg. How gay they were! War seemed very far away. The paths were slippery; I took your arm at times to help you over places and laughed within myself at its reluctance. On the pond the Paris crowd was sliding – old men, women, children, soldiers, all shouting and falling and enjoying themselves hugely.

We walked down the Boule Miche to Notre-Dame, where women were praying for their dead. We peeped in and saw the guttering candles and the wounded saints. Shuddering, we escaped to where the Seine lay blood-red in the winter sunset. What had we to do with death – we who were so young? Presently you spoke of an appointment; all my contentment vanished. Could I see you home? Yes. So we jumped into a taxi. I made a desperate effort not to lose you – what were you doing tonight? You were going to a theatre, but had a spare ticket and invited me to come. "She does care for me a little," I told myself – that thought kept my heart singing after we had parted.

What a silent way you have of entering! I think I noticed it for the first time that night. One never hears you coming; you are absent – one looks again and you are there. Your eyes have a quiet laughter; they seem to know everything and to find amusement in a puzzled world. I can't think that there was ever a time when life perturbed you. If I had told you what was in my mind, I wonder, would it have altered your expression?

You trusted me so much from the very first; is that a good sign for a lover? Strange, that I should have conquered fear in the front-line, should have lived for days quite calmly with sudden death, and yet should tremble before a girl!

I have stopped to glance back through what I have written. Why do I go on writing? You will never read it. I might have said so much to you two hours ago; now it is too late. We have promised to drop each other a line now and then – that was how we put it. Nothing more serious than that! The letter I shall send you will be strictly conventional and not too lengthy – it will be the kind that I might write to any acquaintance of either sex. And yet – yes, that is the thought that troubles me – we may have met and parted for the very last time. Who knows how long one's luck may hold good up Front? The shell which has my name written on it, may be already waiting at some Hun battery. I walk along a trench; there is a rush, a swift impact, blackness – that is the end. It seems indecent that we should have said goodbye so cavalierly – just a shake of the hand, a 'Thank you' for happiness and one of us walks out into Eternity with everything unuttered.

Since you will never read this, I will play a game; I will not send you what I write, but I will speak the truth to you on paper. If I live, perhaps some day, when war is ended, you will receive all your mail at once. If I 'go West' before that can happen, you will never know and will not be hurt by my love. I can dream about you now; in the shell-holes of that unreal world it will seem as if you were really mine.

Perhaps I did not do right by keeping silent; perhaps my silence was false pride. I was talking to one of your friends the other day about soldiers getting married, arguing that such conduct was selfish. She had been quite quiet – hardly interested. Suddenly, with an unexpected violence, she turned. "I wish I had married my man," she said. I learnt her story afterwards. She had been engaged to a French officer and he had been killed. She had joined the Red Cross and ever since has been working her way grimly nearer and nearer to the Front. Did they smile as quietly as we smiled when last they parted?

So many happy times we've had in the last few days –

so much of friendship. I can at least carry the memory of these things back; they are unspoilt by any sadder knowledge. Tonight, this last night, was perfect. We went to our favourite café – the one we visited on that first snowy Sunday. We stopped so long talking over dinner that by the time we reached the opera the first scene was ended. We didn't grieve much. At least, I didn't; the opera was only an excuse for prolonging our time together. How quickly the evening hurried! We were out in the Boulevards again, and it was time to see you home. What fun we had in searching for a non-existent taxi! – then at last we bribed the driver of a private car. Did you expect me to say anything in those last moments? I heard myself talking commonplaces in a voice which did not seem my own. I would speak. I would tell you. We talked. It was too late. Other people were entering the foyer. Of a sudden, after so much intimacy, we became embarrassed. "Goodbye," you said. "Goodbye," I repeated. "You won't forget to write?" You withdrew your hand and nodded. Turning, you ran up the stairs.

I am glad I met you. I am glad of the pain I shall carry back with me. My great loneliness before was that no woman had come into my life. Now I shall be able to think, "I am doing this for her." I shall be able to say, "Perhaps she knew why I did not speak. Perhaps she, too, is remembering?" I shall tell myself stories about you, just as if you were really mine. Your face will be with me, the voice and the memory of your gentleness. I shall be a better soldier because we have met. If I die, I shall die satisfied.

It is very late. Paris will soon be waking. I have to leave

in five hours. I like to think of you as still near me – so near that I could speak with you. You see the telephone is still a temptation, – but then there are no telephones to Paris from the forward guns.

II

IDIDN'T have much time to catch my train, but managed to stop long enough to order you some flowers. They were roses, deep red, the colour of the ones you wore at the opera on our last night. I bought far too many for good taste – I bought the way I felt. At the last minute I forgot to enclose my card, so you won't know who sent them, though probably you'll guess. Once before, if you remember, I sent you flowers and you didn't acknowledge them. Was it because you were afraid to own to sentiment? Until they fade, they'll keep you reminded of me.

Where I am at present the very thought of flowers seems oddly out of place. I look down at myself, plastered with mud, and wonder if I am really the fellow who walked beside you. I'm up as liaison officer; our battalion headquarters are in a dug-out down which the rain pours from the swimming trench outside. Things are pretty lively; the festive Hun is making his presence felt. Our infantry are nervous and expecting a raid.

There's a good deal of shelling of our support trenches and a faint smell of gas. Runners keep coming in with reports, slithering down the stairs and bringing in the mud. A candle gutters at my elbow. I'm sitting on a petrol can with a folded sack for a cushion. By the look of things I shall have to keep awake all night; we've already answered one S.O.S.

How far away you seem – how far everything seems that I have loved. Probably by now, you, too, are doing your duty; I picture you at J———, with your refugee children tucked snugly up in bed. The Huns gas and bomb you sometimes, you told me. I wish selfishly – but no, I'm glad that you are playing the game with us men. I suppose all the pretty clothes are put away – left behind in Paris – and you're wearing your nurse's uniform. You're a captain in A rank, aren't you? Then you're my superior, for I'm only a subaltern. There must be more in you than I have guessed; to have left luxury and come into danger just to look after other people's babies, that took courage. I never thought of you as a soldier when we were in Paris – you were only the most beautiful girl I had ever met. No, more than that – the gentlest and the kindest. There's a religion about you when I think of you as a nurse. There's a sacredness of devotion, which goes deeper than mere beauty.

The blot which ended my last sentence was not entirely my fault. A shell landed at the entrance to our dug-out, killed one runner, wounded two and blew the candle out. We've just finished binding up the two wounded men; the other lies in the passage, covered by a blanket. Poor chap! He's a mere boy and has not been out long. They didn't give him much of a run for his money. Such accidents are largely our own fault. We're always expecting to advance, so we do very little to the trenches which we capture and occupy. The dug-outs faced the right way for the Boche when he held them, but for us they face his shells. C'est la guerre.

It's not taken very long for me to plunge into action. How long? Only four nights since we listened to William Tell and bade each other that unsatisfactory farewell. When I arrived at the railhead on my journey back, I failed to discover my groom with the horses. I phoned up my Division and had to wait till close on midnight before my man arrived. It was a cold ride to the waggon-lines. The road was like glass in places where ditches had overflowed and frozen. We had to walk our beasts a good part of the way; they slithered like cats on the tiles. A hard, chiselled moon was in the sky; the ruined country, forbidding and ghostly, was carved into deep shadows. I learnt that our battery had only moved into its new position that day; consequently everything was at sixes and sevens.

It was nearer three than two in the morning by the time we reached our waggon-lines. The horses were pretty nearly 'all in' with the amount of travelling they had done. The place was a battered village; every barn was full of troops, and for the most part only the walls of the houses were standing. We roused the quartermaster with difficulty; he wasn't very certain as to where our waggon-line officer had his billet. It was too late to go out and search; I unrolled my sleeping-sack and got into it, only removing my boots and tunic. Rather a sudden change from the luxury of the Crillon, the warm baths and the clean-sheeted beds! Do you begin to understand why it is that you seem so far away?

Changes, even more sudden, were in store for me. Shortly after six next morning I was wakened by an orderly; he had come down from the guns to order me to report at once. My toilet didn't take very long – that's one advantage of not undressing. My poor little mare was once more saddled; slung a haversack across my shoulder and away we went along the glassy roads, scrambling and sliding. The orderly informed me on the way what he supposed was the reason for so much haste. One of our subalterns had been sent back of the lines on a course of instruction and another had collected a most beautiful Blighty in the leg. As a consequence our major was short-handed.

I found the battery in a narrow valley. It is one which by name you know well; but names must not be mentioned. A year ago the French made it famous by the fierceness of their fighting. The fighting was all hand-to-hand – so close that bayonets were out of the question, and men stormed the heights with daggers in their mouths. There in the undergrowth the fallen still lie unburied. The snow has covered them for the present, but you can feel their bones beneath your tread. Part way down the valley is a little clump of trees among which our guns are hidden. There are paths leading through the island wood, covered with trellis-work to hide them from aero-plane observation. I left my horses and went on foot the last part of the journey; one does not want to make too many tracks – the snow shows them up too plainly.

I found my major in a hole sunk beneath the ground. "Glad you've come," he said. "Sorry to rush you into harness this way, but it can't be helped. It's our turn to relieve at liaison. I'll give you what information I have and you must be off in quarter of an hour."

I had a hurried breakfast, borrowed some glasses, for mine were with the rest of my kit at the waggon-lines, collected telephonists and went forward. Here I have been for the best part of three days. There isn't much time to think or regret in the army—which is merciful. I am taking pot-luck with the infantry. I have no blankets, no pillow, no nothing; I had to leave everything behind in the hurry. At night I lie down on chicken-wire, spread across supports, and fold my trench-coat beneath my head. It really doesn't matter much not having blankets, for I've had to be up and about all night. The only time that it's safe to sleep is between six and eleven in the morning. I must leave off – something is happening.

– It turned out to be a false alarm. Some one got nervous in the front-line and let off an S.O.S. rocket. We clapped down a barrage on the Hun trenches; if he had intended anything, he changed his mind; All is quiet now, except far to our left, where one can hear occasional machine-gun fire like the clicking of a desultory type-writer. From the enemy's side of No Man's Land flares keep shooting up; they look like taxis speeding through the black-ness. You can weave all kinds of fancies out of our nights if you're in love and have an imagination. Those white flares, appearing, racing, vanishing, seem to me a phantom-city and make me think of Paris.

Sudden memories of you come back – gestures, moods, sayings which I scarcely noticed at the time. Do you remember that night when we went to the Hotel Pavillon together, where the American soldiers meet and you did canteen work? Your job that night was to sell cigarettes. I sat and watched you. The boys came in intending to buy something; they hardly noticed you at first. Then they saw you, stared and tried to spin out an awkward conversation. Decency forbade them to stay too long; but when they had concluded their purchase, they'd return to buy something else. They really returned to get another sight of you. You cushioned your face in your hands while you talked with them; you pretended to be a shop-woman, but quite consciously you fascinated. You fascinated me as well. There was a little hat you wore that night; it was of velvet, and made a slanting line across your forehead, accentuating the fine-ness of your brows. It was the same hat that you wore when we met so briefly in America.

What are you? You are drifting away from me, becoming unreal already. I can't associate you with this place of imminent death – you are so much alive. Did you care for me at all, even for a moment? Did you ever picture the life to which I was going? Was I only an incident – some one transiently amusing, and perhaps a little pleasant? We never spoke of what lay before or behind – we merely enjoyed our handful of hours. But for me there was always poignancy in our happiness. The thought was constantly with me of our parting. Something within me kept warning, "It is the end – the end – the end." If I had only met you earlier, in the days before war started, I

27

could have made love to you honourably. But not now. I turn my head and look out into the passage across my shoulder; I see the boots, the form beneath the blanket, the stretcher. He was a man once; in a second of time what lies there was all that was left. Perhaps he, too, loved a girl. Perhaps he told her. How much better if he had kept silent. And yet – "I wish I had married my man," your friend said. It's a problem. Self-interest dictates that I should tell you. That choice might be more righteous than silence; it depends on you. But because the choice would be selfish I distrust it.

Here is another letter which will never reach you. The letter you will get will be quite different. I shall address you by your surname, tell you briefly that I'm back in the line, and ask how things are going with you. I wonder, will you write? When I asked you to do so, was that embarrassed nod of your head a polite evasion of a refusal? I can see you now as you ran up the stairs. You didn't look back. Had you stayed a moment longer I might have spoken the words which were better left unsaid. I think you knew that.

It's nearly morning. Nothing will happen. I'm going to lie down and get a little rest.

III

THE mail has just come in. It was brought up on the ammunition limbers. We heard the cry, " Mail up,'" and then the running feet of the men. It's queer to think how far those letters travel and how safely they arrive. They are brought up to us under shell-fire, through gas, by runners, pack animals, limbers. Since no movement is allowed near the guns by day, they invariably reach us at night. Before ever they can be distributed, the ammunition has to be unloaded so that the teams may get out of range. That accounts for the speed with which the men work. They form a chain, and pass the shells swiftly to the gun-pits. Until everything is safely stored away the pages from their mothers, wives and sweethearts must wait. When the last shell has been laid in its rack, they scramble to the sergeant-major's dug-out. He crouches over the bag by the light of the candle and reads aloud the name on each envelope or parcel. Finally the bag is empty. He turns it upside down and shakes it. There will be no more news from home till next night. The crowd scatters; the blackness becomes again lonely.

We officers have to sit still and wait for our letters to be brought to us by our servants. It's a sore trial to our patience – part of the price we pay for our rank. Tonight I made sure I should hear from you. At the cry, "Mail up," I forsook my dignity and went out on the pretence of seeing that the teams were clear of the position. It was such a night; the stars and snow were like silver inlaid in ebony. From the gun-pits came the glow of fires. Men were already sitting round them in silence, reading by the light of the jumping flames. The frost on the duck-board crackled beneath my tread. War seemed to have ceased for a little while; for a little while memories travelled back to affections and quiet.

My servant met me with a bundle of letters. "The officers. Will you take them, sir?"

I returned to the hole in the ground which we call our mess, and sorted them out on the table. At a glance I saw that there was nothing from you – my three letters were in known handwritings. A queer way to tell! You mean more to me than anyone in the world, yet I have never seen your handwriting. That brings home to me vividly how much we are strangers.

Every one in our mess has something tonight. Jack Holt has made the biggest haul; there are four from his wife. He married her in a hurry two years ago. He'd only known her a week, I understand. They had a four days' honeymoon; then he came to France. He's spent about thirty days with her in his entire life. I never knew a man more in love with anybody; I'm his best pal, so he tells me about her. Our major got only one letter. His girl is, like you, in a French Hospital. I have an idea that she plays him up sometimes. It's incredible that anyone should trifle with our major. He doesn't look very pleased; he's puckering his brows. Then there's Bill Lane; he didn't come off so badly. He's a nervous kind of chap and, despite that, plucky. His girl is in England. He plans to marry her on his next leave. He's most frightfully worried lest a shell should get him before that happens; nevertheless, he plays the game to the limit with the best of us. He's smiling now as he turns his pages. Poor old thing, for once his mind is at rest; he's happy. And then there's Stephen, our expert draughtsman. No one ever writes to him. He's handsome and the best of fellows. He shows no excitement when our letters are distributed. He expects nothing. While we read ours, he bends where the light spills over the table, and goes on ruling arcs into his map.

Why didn't you write to me? I had counted the days and made allowances for delays. A letter might have come yesterday; tonight it seemed certain. I form so many conjectures – the old ones which lovers have fashioned so many times to dispel their doubts. You were busy. You did write, but forgot to post it. You posted it, and it's held up in the transit. Then there are other conjectures of another kind: that you do not care; that the knowledge that I care would come to you as a surprise; that it is the knowledge that I care that keeps you from writing. I close my eyes and concentrate my memories; your face grows clear to me again. When I remember you like that I feel your kindness. You may not care, but you are not careless; I could make you care if I liked. To have known you as I have is more

31

than I had counted on, more than I deserved. To have had love come to one in the midst of a war, was more than could have been expected. All my life I had waited for that; then, when one had sacrificed so many human affections, it happened. It was a gift from the gods. Though you may never know, I ought to be contented.

In this strange world, where courage masquerades as duty, we have left all hope behind. To hope too much is to court cowardice. To be brave one should live a day at a time. In the past I was so selfish, so full of plans for happiness. I wanted to live so strongly, to be so much, to do so much, to hold the whole world in my hands. I had my future planned out for forty years. I felt as though the destiny of all the generations depended on what I should do with my time. And then this war came. I had never dreamt of fighting. The thought that I should ever kill anybody was inconceivable; it was worse than that – it was a terror. One had to sink personality and ambition; throw aside everything for which one had been trained; take up a way of life which was abhorrent to one's nature; place oneself in a position where one must be inefficient; and stand the strong chance of dying shortly, in a manner which seemed incommensurately obscure and out of proportion ghastly. And why? Because Calvary had repeated itself; after two thousand years to die for others had become again worthwhile.

I must not entertain hopes about you. To do so would be weakening. You have happened in my life – that should be sufficient. To have snatched one last glimpse of loyalty should make me braver; it should be like the sacrament pressed

32

against the lips of those about to die. I don't think I will write to you any more, my dear. These unposted letters, written out of loneliness, are becoming a luxury which is dangerous. They make the future seem too valuable. I begin to realize how sweet life is – how glorious we could make it. I would rather be at rest within myself if I am called upon to say goodbye. You ran up the stairs without turning your head when we parted. That's the way I would prefer to go out of life.

IV

A LETTER from you! Such a jolly letter, so full of yourself! It's just as though you were at my elbow and I could hear your voice. It's as though you let me take your arm again, the way I did in the Luxembourg Gardens to help you over the slippery places. What a reluctant, stiffly proper arm it was on that first occasion. But your letter! I've read it how many times? I can't count. I think I know it all by heart, and yet I keep on turning back to my, favourite passages. There's the one in which you describe your first introduction to the town of J———. How it was night, every light extinguished and the streets a stagnant river of blackness – no sound, no life, a habitation of the dead. Then the sudden commotion in the sky, the rattle of machine-guns, the glare of a plane descending in flames and the crash of bombs on the house-tops. Weren't you frightened? There's no hint of fear in your letter. "From my selfish point of view," you write, "it was the best thing that could have happened. It taught me in an instant how badly

I was needed there." A gallant way of being selfish! You're just as exultant over your job as we men in the front-line; it's the immense chance for sacrifice that intrigues one. I suppose even in peace-times the chance was always there only one's eyes were blinded. Perhaps the sacrifice demanded wasn't large enough.

I ought to be vastly concerned at the risks you are taking. I'm not; I'm too glad that your spirit should be kindled by danger. To save France, Joan of Arc charged on horseback into battle. You go with less drama, but with an equal heroism. Your charger is a Ford car. You have exchanged your armour for a uniform of the Croix Rouge Américaine. You don't kill; you rescue children. Frankly I prefer your work. If you could look over my shoulder, you would laugh quietly and say that I make too much of what you are doing – that it's really very ordinary. It's ordinary here in France, I grant you. In France laying down one's life for some one else has become a habit. But it wasn't a habit where you came from. In Fifth Avenue it wouldn't have been difficult to have played safe.

What a romance! As a rule, you Americans aren't a romantic nation. You've such terrific common sense. Now you, for instance, who have your limousines and your several houses, come three thousand miles to do a servant's work and perhaps to die, yet you don't seem to thrill at yourself. You belittle your heroism by taking it utterly for granted. The French are so different. Their feet are never on the ground; they're forever aeroplaning. They view their present in the light of history and see their blood pouring like a crimson tide down the future ages. We English are quite conscious of our splendour, only we don't talk about it. We do magnificent things and voice them in the language of stable-boys. We're so terribly afraid of self-praise and sentiment. We feel intensely, but we keep up a pretence of carelessness. You Americans are too honest for pretence. You go in for rescuing lives with the same determination that you apply to tangoing, only somehow you don't see the difference. It's the determination with which you set about a job that fascinates you; you don't congratulate yourselves on the job itself. You never lose your heads.

I spoke of sentiment just now and how we English hate it and try to disguise it. Take myself. Why didn't I propose to you? Because I was afraid of trading on your sentiment. It's a difficult thing for a girl to refuse a man who is going back into the line. She may easily be deceived into a belief that she loves him, whereas her only feeling may be pity for him. So out of shame of sentiment I refused to make love to you, yet because of sentiment I sit in dirty kennels putting an immense deal of sentiment down on paper – all to no purpose.

Life has always puzzled me; before the war I used to be afraid of it. I used to hover between decisions, look too far ahead and hesitate to achieve. Military discipline has given me a purpose – to live bravely, dare cheerfully and, if need be, to die gratefully. So you see how meeting you has upset my plans. You can't love a woman and not gaze into the future. You can't feel the need of her and be resigned to die.

And yet, the romance! That stirs me. It's mediaeval. It has all the accompaniments of legend. Most men meet their wives at tennis-parties, court them at theatres and marry them in a church. Not so you and I. We meet by accident in America at a point of parting; then again in Paris without design. We say goodbye, both going to do a soldier's work. We are young, and the world should lie before us; but we jeopardize love, youth and the world for an ideal which consumes us. Most triumphant of all, we would not have things otherwise. By a strange logic I kill and you cure, yet both our tasks are compatible with the same purpose. In putrescence and destruction unimaginable your scribbled pages flutter to me, and mine – some of them reach you, but not all that I write. Our spirits rise above the pity and the squalor. The vilest thing in history is happening about us; but, because we are here to combat it, our spirits grow in stature. Isn't that romance? Doesn't it thrill you, my common-sense little American?

And how do you think your letter arrived – the first letter that you ever wrote me? There's a long ridge runs along the valley, very steep and very difficult to climb. It's glassy with frozen snow at present; there are caved-in trenches running straight up its side. Scattered beneath the bushes dead men lie of past and unrecorded offences. Whether Huns or Frenchmen, after a year they look the same; only their uniforms mark the difference. At the top of the ridge are more trenches – a network of them. They are in full sight of the enemy, and all of them decayed. The trench which I occupy is half-way down the slope; it can only be approached by night or under cover of the mist of early morning. There's an old dug-out, which has been partly bombed, and at the top of it a spy-hole. Through the spy-hole my telescope is placed, and I am continually watching for any sign of movement in the Hun country. Yesterday the mist parted suddenly, and I caught sight of the enemy working. I guessed the map-location, telephoned back to the guns and waited for the mist to part again. I caught the Boche in the open with shrapnel. They ran and I followed them, lengthening my range. There was wire between them and safety; they tried to scramble through it, under it, over it, and there I nailed them. I counted ten dead men; an equal number must have been wounded. In peace-times to have beaten a dog would have pained me. Here to kill men does not trouble my conscience. Curious! I sit like God in hiding, watching the world and arbitrarily dictating who shall be the next to die.

It was here that your letter reached me very early in the morning. My servant brought it with him as he sneaked in with the rations. I read it, as I'm writing this, with one eye on the enemy and the other on your pages. Probably some Hun artilleryman behind the mist is doing very much the same. He wants to live just as much as I do; he's just as anxious to meet his girl again. He bears me no enmity, yet if I gave him the chance he would dispassionately kill me. The chief horror of our modern Warfare is that it is so anonymous and mechanical. One rarely sees the hand that strikes. Cromwell's Ironsides faced their opponents; they went into battle chanting the Psalms of David. We steal out of our trenches behind a smoke-barrage and do all our slaughtering in silence.

I can't focus you any more than I can focus myself. In Paris we neither recognized in each other the kind of persons that we really were. I met you with buttons shined; we chattered socially, were easily shocked and dined sedately. You were perishably dressed; I was concerned for you if we couldn't find a taxi or if it rained. Now I take my chances and wait long hours to destroy, while you wade through the back-wash of an army. We can't explain ourselves. But, after so much that was trivial, isn't it good to be doing something strong at last?

The mist is rising. I shall have to keep a sharper look-out. Here's another letter to keep until that future day when war is ended and I am free to tell you. So goodbye, my Joan of Arc, with your "flivver," your pale rose beauty and your Croix Rouge Américaine. Joan saw her visions in the woods about Domrémy – you in the hot-house palaces of New York. You both answered the call of duty; your spirit is the same, though centuries divide you.

V

I HAVE not heard from you for three weeks – not since that first letter. I have no right to expect you to write to me. Why should you? So far as you were aware, I was only a passer-by. If I had wanted to be more to you, I could have put the matter to the test. If I had spoken to you on that last night. Yes, and if I had spoken what good would it have done to either of us? I don't see how you could have accepted me. And yet—I wish I knew that you felt the need of me. In the loneliness of this existence the knowledge that there is one woman who cares supremely helps.

I stop to read what I have written. It is unmanly. It is self-pity – the worst enemy that a soldier can have. The only way one can endure is to be forgetful of self – to consider one's body, one's pain, everything personal as of no account. The game – the establishing of the ideal for which we fight – is the only thing that matters.

There comes a point in the career of every fighting man

when he can endure no further. He may be perfectly healthy, but he knows that the day is surely coming when he will break. It may not come for a long time; but the certainty that the break is coming fills him with dread. Inadvertently he betrays this dread in little ways. Officers who have trusted him begin to watch him – they begin to doubt his courage.

We had such a man on our B.C. party. The B.C. party consists of expert signallers and linesmen, chosen out of the battery for their pluck. As the English say, they have to be 'stout' fellows. Their job is to go forward and sometimes over the top with the observing officer to direct fire. At all costs and at whatever risks, they have to keep up the communications with the battery. If the line goes down no matter how bad the shelling, your linesmen are expected to go out and mend it. This man of whom I speak was a linesman. He'd been in the war from the first and had made a record for his daring. He had stood the racket for two years, then his nerve began to go from him. We wouldn't believe it at first; soon it became patent to everybody. His eyes would become vague. You could see him making an effort not to run. He quivered like a high-strung horse under shell-fire. Of course the just thing would have been to have sent him out; but we had had too many casualties and couldn't spare him. In such cases the last thing one dares to do is to show pity. Pity is contagious. The army expects every man to do his duty; it takes no excuses, and only notices him when he fails. So this poor chap, who had been a hero, had to watch himself hourly becoming a coward. Worse still, he was kept wondering just how many of us knew it. He must have been very brave, for he played the game to the end.

We were in a position where the Hun pounded us day and night. The B.C. party's quarters were under a ruined house which might fall at any moment. The enemy had already scored several direct hits on it. Suddenly, in the middle of a strafe, he began to undress. When he was asked what he was doing, he paid no attention. When he'd got rid of every stitch of clothing, he dashed out into the area where the shells were falling. He was stark mad.

That's why one must beware of self-pity. I mustn't think of you too often. I must act as though we had never met. I must –

But this is foolishness – one can't get rid of memory. Since I can't forget you, I must make your memory a help. Who was it said – Epictetus, wasn't it? – that every burden has two handles: one by which it can be carried, and one by which it cannot? The wise man finds the handle by which he can carry his burdens. Here's the way in which I'm going to make my love for you help. At the end of the war, if I survive, I'll seek you out; that promise shall be my goal. Meanwhile I'll cease to keep in touch with you. We're both engaged upon an adventure equally lonely and too fine to be disturbed by selfishness.

A week ago, by the most extraordinary of accidents, I found a book which confirms me in this decision. There was some enemy front-line wire that had to be cut before our infantry made their attack; it was impossible by consulting contours on the map to say from what point one could view it – you cut wire by bursting shrapnel just over it and stripping it off the stakes by the impact of the bullets. To do this each round ought to be observed. There was great competition among the officers of our brigade as to who should get the credit of having done the job. Our only chance was to wander about the trenches and out into No Man's Land, if need be, till we struck a point which had been wrongly put in on the map, from which our line of vision would clear the crest and let us see the entanglements on the other side.

I had a hunch that I knew a place from which I could see it. It was a smashed-in Hun gun-pit in the debatable ground between Fritzie's and our own front-line. There was a sap leading to it, but it was very shallow. Any movement there was certain to attract the enemy snipers. One of them, whom our Chaps had nicknamed 'Little Willie,' made this sap his speciality. In order that I might not afford him a target, I got up very early so as to sneak in when the mist was on the ground. I took one telephonist with me and proposed to spend my day there, do my job and get out when night fell.

To cut a long story short, I got into the gun-pit without being detected. It was in a beastly mess and had evidently been the scene of fierce fighting. There was a pile of dead Germans before the entrance, as though our fellows had caught them as they tried to rush out. They lay there with their arms across their faces, shielding their eyes, in every sort of pitiful attitude. I'd made a bad bet about the gun-pit, for it was choked with debris and impossible to enter. There was a dug-out by the side, however, with stairs leading down; though the timbers were all slantwise, it was possible to squeeze past, and it gave us concealment. The visibility was still wretched, so, having nothing better to do, we began to investigate.

At the bottom of the stairs there was a shored-up chamber with two bunks made of a chicken wire. Leading off to the right was a-tunnel, so knocked about that you had to go on your hands and knees to pass through it. When you're in a place of this kind it's always well to employ your leisure in trying to find another exit. You may need it. One shell, well directed, would seal up your entrance. So down on our hands and knees we went to see where the tunnel led. It wasn't a very pleasant business, for in falling the dirt had buried quite a number of the old inhabitants; as a consequence, our crawling was rather up hill and down dale. I suppose we must have gone twenty yards when we came to a second chamber. The air was foul with decay and damp. There was a glimmer of light far up above us, which evidently came from a caved-in exit. I turned on my flash-light. What I saw was startling.

A big Prussian was sitting on the edge of his bunk. He must have been dead three weeks; but he looked life-like. On the floor was a book which had fallen from his hand. I picked it up. Incongruously enough, its binding was preserved by a newspaper cover. I glanced at the title: 'The Research Magnificent' by H. G. Wells. I glanced through the pages; the first thing I struck was a marked passage with some comment scrawled against it in German. The passage read, "Like all of us he had been prepared to take life in a certain way and life had taken him, as it takes all of us, in an entirely different way. He had been ready for noble deeds..." At that point the marking ended. I looked at this philosopher, forgotten and entombed deep underground. His beard had grown, his eyes were sunken, his mouth was open, his head lolled in an imbecile fashion. Across his temple was a wide gash where the fragment of a bomb had struck him. I seemed to hear the words ticking behind his forehead, "He had been ready for noble deeds. Life had taken him, as it takes all of us, in an entirely different and unexpected way." I felt sick with a kind of physical sorrow—not for him in particular, but for all the world. After that, the crawl back across the hills and dales of the pitch-black tunnel was horrible.

I sat on the topmost stairs at the entrance and turned the pages. I kept wondering how the Prussian had come by a novel that has only been published since hostilities commenced. Then I discovered. Other passages were marked; beside the markings were pencilled comments, some of them in English, some in German, but in different hands. As I studied the passages I found that most of them had reference to fear and its conquest. 'The beginning of all aristocracy is the subjugation of fear.' This was heavily underlined.

And again this passage, 'When I was a boy I thought I would conquer fear for good and all. It is not to be done that way. One might as well dream of having dinner for the rest of one's life. Each time and always I find that it has to be conquered afresh.' The Englishman's pencilled comment is very typical, 'Quite so. But you oughtn't to admit it.' The comment of the Prussian, who killed the English owner and then re-edited his reflections, fills the entire margin and runs over on to the next page. It is too guttural for my comprehension.

Here is the last section. The German keeps silent this time, but the Englishman's comment makes it worth recording. The marked portion reads as follows: 'In his younger days Benham had regarded fear as a shameful secret and as a thing to be got rid of altogether. It seemed to him that to feel fear was to fall short of aristocracy. But as he emerged from the egotism of adolescence he came to realize that every one feels fear, and your true aristocrat is not one who has eliminated, but one who controls and ignores it.' The English-man's note is, "Bravo, old cock! Now you're talking!"

The mist had not cleared and showed no sign of clearing, so there in No Man's Land on this winter's morning I gave myself up to studying the problem of noble living as worked out in the career of an individual named Benham.

Have you ever caught a sudden reflection of yourself and thought, "What an absurd person! Good Lord, can I be like that?" For a moment you judge yourself without affection, as you would a stranger. That's the way I felt in the reading of this book.

This Benham was a prig in the most charitable sense of the word. I pictured him with a white faced and bulging forehead – too many brains and too little body. At an early date he discovered that there was something wrong with himself, but he attributed the reason to a lack of harmony in the world. He at once conceived that the only way to mend himself was to set about mending the world. Of course the world refused to be mended – it always does. It invariably crucifies its Christs. This Benham actually dreamt that he might be a second Christ – a kind of god-man who, by right of intellect rather than love, could force nations into magnamity. The trouble was that in his own small, daily decisions he was neither magnanimous nor god-like; he wasn't even decided. He was afraid; though he made heroic efforts, he never conquered fear to the day of his death. He had no sympathy with children, but he babbled with swimming eyes about his own childhood. He could make women love him, but he always coveted the affection that was out of sight; he had no patience to hold the affection he had won. He yearned to save men in masses, but made no attempt to save the neighbour who was within reach. Always, always he wasted his good impulses on abstractions. He was eternally educating himself for a splendid self-abnegation which he never had the grit to accomplish. Instead of achieving an isolated kindness, he embittered himself with the sorrow of continents. His dream was to make himself king of the world; in the pursuit of his dream he pushed aside every tender and ordinary human affection. He died a bankrupt at heart, absurdly fluttering a waiter's napkin to prevent soldiers from firing on rioters. On the charger of his imagination he fancied himself as riding through Time, upholding a banner woven from the clouds. Actually all he has been doing was waving a waiter's napkin at Jupiter, to prevent him from hurling thunderbolts. When Jupiter failed to obey him he was extraordinarily annoyed.

I make fun of this fantastic Benham, but in past days I was so very unlike him. If it comes to that there are streaks of Benham in me now. I write you letters which you will never receive, recording the fact that I love you; but I fail to

47

tell you. I persuade myself as Benham would have persuaded himself, that it is honest and fine not to confess. I don't do the passionately human thing – the thing that Jack Holt did when he won his wife. I act idealistically but, God knows, I'm by no means certain of my motives. You see I have always been able to view every question from at least a dozen sides. I speculate where a baser man would act; it is my infirmity. Life has gone by me. No, not gone; it went by me until this war broke out.

It went by me in such curious ways. Now that I live constantly in the presence of death I can see why life eluded me; I was afraid of soiling my dreams with reality. As my father's son I got into Parliament as soon as I left Oxford; I believed that I could solve the problem of poverty in a decade. I discovered that politics are employed for personal ends; that statesmen usually think nationally only when votes are necessary. In protest I resigned my seat and went to live in the slums for a while. There I learnt that poverty is disturbingly contented, and that philanthropy is as untidy as it is unrewarding. Goaded by fierce contempt for self-complacency, I went to Russia to sympathize with the revolution that was brewing. Again I undeceived myself. My sympathy was not wanted. I found young men plucking out their eyes, posing as martyrs, and saying that the Czar had blinded them. There are people in the world who are born to mutilate themselves and invariably blame someone else. Don't you see how I was learning that it isn't the thing you plan to do, but the thing you are inside yourself that counts? And life, as I say, was going by while I, in my earnestness that future centuries might be better, was neglecting the dear, simple, daily loyalties.

Then this war broke out, stripping us of our sham refinements and clothing us in the armour of duty. We hadn't known how to live wisely; God restored to us the chance to die for something worthy. He'd grown tired of seeing us charging windmills, so He set over against us the mustered hosts of hell. How real everything has become of late! All the ghosts of distrust and derision have vanished. Men's souls gleam in their eyes. We have regained the old primitive strength of the saints to strike sin where we find it. We no longer doubt when the sky is overshadowed that heaven floats above the clouds.

'Like all of us he had been prepared to take life in a certain way and life had taken him, as it takes all of us, in an entirely different way. He had been ready for noble deeds...' As I sat there in hiding in No Man's Land, I reflected on these words. The Prussian had pondered them before he died, and the Englishman who had possessed the book before that. They both had tried, and they were enemies. In the old days I would have puzzled over this inconsistency, striving vainly to find a reconciling argument. Now, in the larger kindness which I have gained, I forgot the motive in remembering the sacrifice. I wanted the Prussian to know that I felt like that.

The mist had not cleared, and it was lunch-time. Crawling through the tunnel, I re-entered the dismal chamber and placed a portion of my meal beside him. Death had eliminated enmity. It was as thought we had broken bread together.

VI

A T last a letter, and a long letter. I found it at the guns, when I got back from up front this morning. It's exactly the kind of day when one would expect one's luck to change. The skies are high and fleecy; the mud is drying up; there's a touch of premature spring in the air. It's the kind of day when one expects to find primroses in London; and in New York – what kind of flowers do they sell in the street there? Some day, when war is over, you shall take me down Fifth Avenue and we'll find out. It's the kind of day when a man plans and looks ahead, and feels in his bones that he's going to live forever.

By the time we meet in New York, the clothes that you wore in Paris will be out of fashion. I wonder how you'll be dressed. Do you think, just to please me, you might–? But no, that's asking too much. No girl would wear clothes two summers old to please any man.

So you've seen something of what war is like! You can't tell me very plainly, but I can read between the lines and guess. A

50

month ago we heard rumours that the Huns had made a break in a sector held by the French. It never occurred to me that you might be there. Thank God, it didn't. It's easy to be brave for one's self, but to have known that you were in danger would have been intolerable. You remember that I protested in Paris that they were placing your hospital too near to the front-line. I nearly made you angry with protesting; you were so eager to share the game with us men. I remember how you said "Our lives are of less value than you men's – there are more of us in the world. If they can afford to let you get killed, why shouldn't we be allowed to take our chance of death?" I'm proud of you – immensely proud.

I understand now the reason for your long silence. After the order came out for the evacuation of the civil population you, who remained behind, were not allowed to write. By all accounts, even if you had been allowed, you were too busy. I'm trying to picture all the hazard of those exciting days when the Huns were breaking through, and nobody knew to what depth. I can see you racing to and fro in your Ford ambulance, carrying your babies out of the shelled town and, when that was done, volunteering to stay behind in the thick of it to tend the wounded. You've seen troops marching up singing, with the certainty in their hearts that they were going to die. You've stood by the road and cheered them; they blew kisses to you, laughing gaily, and you blew kisses back. For many of them you were the last woman they would see in this world. How simple and happy everything becomes in the presence of a great sacrifice! I can see you in your uniform of the Croix

Rouge Américaine, the white veil blowing back and your young face ecstatic, while all in front, in an abandon of heroic exaltation, the ceaseless tide of doomed men flowed by. You've seen that same tide return – the crimson ripples of what was left of it: me without hands, or eyes or legs, limping, carried on stretchers, hurried in the ambulance. I think the most poignant thing you've told me is of the man without lips who pressed your dress against his bandages in gratefulness. Could I see you I should find you changed, you say; the sleepless nights have done their work. I expect I should find you changed – as metal is tried in the furnace.

So your friend at last has had her desire. I shall never forget the sharp whisper, like a sob stifled, in which she said "I wish I had married my man." Since her lover was killed in action, she was always thrusting forward, nearer and nearer to the zone of danger. She must be happy now that she has shared his end. Don't you think there was a touch of conscience in her obsession? Perhaps he had asked her to marry him before he went and she refused him. It seemed to me like that. It was fine of her to protect the dying poilu with her body from the falling shells. Fine and fruitless! As you say, he would have died anyhow. The sheer wastefulness of her death makes it even more heroic.

She did not look that type of girl. She impressed me at first as being hard and managing and selfish; there was too much drive in her character. Probably she wasn't always like that. The one and only time that she betrayed her inner gentleness was when she said, "I wish I had married my man." You may call war damnable, a vile misuse of courage – there is nothing too bad that can be said about it – and yet, as nothing else does, it teaches us how to die for our friends. It has a knack, which peace had never learned, of uncovering the splendour of commonplace persons.

And now you're again in comparative safety. I wonder how comparative. You're once again nursing refugee babies behind the lines. Little Gaston, you say, is your favourite. He's six days old, has the face of an old man of eighty and the most heavenly blues eyes. You live in an old *caserne* and, "it's dreadfully draughty and most horribly unsanitary," and you're terrifically happy.

Shall I tell you a secret? When I was with you in Paris I made up my mind that you wouldn't stick this work. It was obvious to me, when you spoke of 'going up the line,' that you hadn't the foggiest notion of to what you were going. You looked so delicate, so frail, so beautiful. You'd never had to work in your life. You'd been dressed and conveyed from point to point, and hadn't the least conception of the patience that it takes to do anything well. There was an expensive look of innocence about you that one doesn't associate with the ghastly knowledge of battle-fields. You hadn't realized the horror of the Western Front – no, nor the glory of it; you had too complete an air of rest. Often as I sat beside you at a theatre or in a café the thought would come to me, "How will all these men who are laughing and enjoying themselves look in six months' time?" I could see them lying out in No Man's Land, little sacks that had been dropped from a waggon. I could see them with their faces hideously transformed, staring up unseeing at the changing sky. She doesn't know these things, I thought. She must never know them. Like every man who loves a woman, the desire of my heart was to shut you up in a cage of unreality. How wrong I should have been, for then your flower-body would never have become the scabbard of the sword of compassion. You are a woman for a soldier now; you were a plaything then.

You spoke of this once, I remember, saying how difficult it was to have been born rich. Everything had been done; you weren't supposed to do anything. You wanted – you didn't know what you wanted but it must be something satisfying and splendid. Just to slip into matrimony and be your mother all over again wasn't satisfying; you wanted to get your feet off the ground, to aeroplane, to bump your head against the stars, to crash and set out afresh in quest of the playground of celestial bodies. You achieved all this in a better way when you stayed in the city pounded by Hun shells, and smiled at the boys who marched up to die.

Do we really suffer? I doubt it. Mud and wounds and torture and discomfort, what do they matter when the spirit flames so high? You and I, both in our separate ways, were afraid of life; now that were are bankrupt in a righteous cause we are contented. It's a gallant world – the more gallant because we are parted; for me that is the supreme sacrifice. One gets a lust for saying "No" to oneself when once one starts the habit; one gets scientifically curious to discover just what are the limits to one's self denial.

When you write of children, I think I have reached mine. I sit here behind the gun-pits, picturing your arms about the little bodies and the little heads pressed against your breast. You're a girl, so slim, so much like sculpted ivory. There's an ethereal and indefinable purity about you. When I picture you with the little children, I think of the future which may never be ours. For the moment I becomes rebellious. Dead men's children are their only certain immortality. I have seen so many men rise up in the morning and lie still at night.

Such thoughts are unpardonable. They have no right to be set down.

"Goodbye," you write. "Because I have seen what war is like, I beg you to take special care of yourself. Don't run more risks than you can help." But, my dear, to run risks one is supposed to avoid is what I am here for. To do more than is expected of one is the proof of a good soldier. I beg you, however, not to stay in any more shelled towns so long as there's a decent chance to get out.

VII

MY mind is full of you today. I have been trying to remember your face, the tones of your voice – all the things that make you you so essentially. At this distance, with so little hope of seeing you till war is ended, I grow afraid les my imaginings should overlay the person you are really. You know how often it is with the Old Masters when they begin to fade; some lesser man takes in hand to restore the Masters' work and alters the whole sincerity of what was intended. I want you to be so perfect in my memory that I stand the risk of making you inhuman.

At first, when I fell in love with you, I almost resented your intrusion; not that you did actually intrude, for even up to this day you have not so much as raised your little finger. If I stopped writing for any reason, I should not hear from you again. You were like La Giaconda in your smiling aloofness. You lure without effort and are silent.

I wanted to be so string in this war, so single of purpose,

and brave for hardship. I didn't want to have any regrets if the hour came for the final sacrifice. Long ago, when we all went about our own selfish business of money-gathering and fame-getting, I used to distrust love as a kind of sickness, and yet all the while – I must tell the truth – I longed for it desperately. Love always avoided me. I was too intent on my career. There was such big things to do with life. "Love will come later," I told myself, "when I have time." I have always been wantonly an idealist, forgoing the things I might have had for the things which are out of sight. I wanted to have something so worth giving to a woman; perhaps that was why I was willing to delay.

And then this war came. I thanked God that I was free to take my chances without jeopardizing the happiness of another. For two years I've stood it, running my risks alone; and now there's you.

In the old days I used to watch attacks with mixed sensations. I used to look at dead men, wondering whether they had children. It wasn't a dead man that I saw on a battle-field, but the tragedy of unborn children. I felt that tragedy for myself; I hungered to have a youngster who would be myself over again long after I was dead. That was the selfish part of me – the cry-baby part, if you like; the part that never grows any older than when a mother used to nurse it. That part waited half-starved inside me, just as the refugee children wait for your coming. It ceased crying for the first time when I had met you. One gets tired at this fighting-game – tired of enduring, tired of being cruel, tired of the effort to be brave. Then a quaint little picture forms in my brain of you and me alone in a darkened room. There's a fire burning. You're sitting in a great arm-chair; I'm crouched like a child on the floor beside you, my head against your knees and your hands for my toys. Not a soldier's dream! But one grows weary of being strong; once wants to be loved so badly, just once while there is time.

There are absurd words to write you. By no hint have I warned you that you are all my life. You may not care for me; I have no reason to suppose that you do.

And yet, for men in the mass, love seems by no means rare. There's hardly a driver or a gunner in my battery who has not his Flo or his Dorothy. I have to censor their letters, so I'm pretty well acquainted with the heart-affairs of my men. Some of them are regular Don Juans, making the same protestations of undying affection in half a dozen different directions. Most of the letters bear the mystic letters S.W.A.K. – which means, being interpreted, 'Sealed With A Kiss' – a totally inaccurate statement, since sealing them is part of my duty.

Poor lads, how many of them have written that lie, 'Sealed With A Kiss' – written it for the last time for some girl to pin her heart to.

I want you in such a childish sort of way today – not the way in which a man usually wants a woman. It's the feel of you I need, the protection, the security – the sure knowledge that I am yours, whatever happens. There's a verse of Matthew Arnold's I remember; I used rather to sneer at him when I read it; but now I understand:

Come to me in my dreams, and then
By day I shall be well again;
For then the night will more than pay
The hopeless longing of the day.

I suppose if you had met Matthew Arnold the moment after
he had written those lines, he would have looked self-contained
and icy. To the outside world he seems always to have appeared
a perambulating refrigerator. And yet he could cry out like that
– like a child who has wakened in the night and is lonely.

A child who has wakened in the night and is lonely! That's what I
am. I was asleep; you stole to my bed and roused me, and now
you've gone away. It's you that I want – the feel of your hands
touching mine in the darkness and your arms about me.

If I give way like this I shall be telling you, and I must not
tell. I must forget, as you have, perhaps. I must externalize
myself – see myself as I am – a mere, unimportant cog in a
vast machine which is struggling for the world's redemption.
Some one who, without altering the course of nations, may be
dead tomorrow. A man, muddy, unwashed, unpleasing, sitting
in the chaos of an old battle-field and doing his infinitesimal
share. *My share!* That's what I must remember. If you stop
me from doing my share, you must be forgotten. There are
other men here who might remember – men with wives and
sweethearts and children. None of us must weaken; none of
us must remember. We must got forward and always forward,
dragging in our guns along barraged roads, holding life cheap

for the cause in which we fight, defeating hell even though we have to do it with our naked flesh.

And yet – what use does pretence serve? – in each of our hearts there's a little boy, who whimpers in his bed and pushes back the darkness with his puny hands. That may be; but thank God, our faces are stern and don't show it.

VIII

I'M afraid I've been acting like the traditional Englishman; you're the greatest pleasure I have and I've been taking you sadly. It isn't much of a compliment to you and I must stop it. Unhappiness is a form of disloyalty. If you trace it back far enough it's irreligion, for it is based on a doubt as to the goodness of God's world. I think a tragic chap must always lose what he's after; he jolly well deserves to lose it.

In Thomas Hardy's novel when a fellow comes a cropper he calls it Fate. "It has to be," he says. Well, there's where I disagree; I don't call it Fate – I call it lack of guts. A Hardy hero, when he falls in love with a girl, immediately begins to suspect that he isn't in love. He fools along with her, blowing cold and hot, until, another fellow turns up, whereupon he discovers that he wants her immensely, and she discovers that she'd like to experiment in another direction. He then gets desperate, and instead of playing the man emigrates and leaves a clear field for his rival. The girl marries Number Two on the rebound, but instead of playing fair by him sentimentalizes over the absent Number One. Of course she makes a mess of her married life, she walks forward to meet the future with her face turned towards the past. She walks into a lot of things and gets bruised all over through not looking where's she's going. When she has sufficiently bruised herself, Number One comes back from the Colonies and finds that he doesn't want her – she's walked into two many obstacles in his absence. Neither of them blames the other. 'It had to be.' They say sorrowfully; and there the book ends.

Hardy is a very fine writer, but I wish he'd be honest. Life becomes a mucky affair when people are cowards. Thank God, however shoddy we may have been in the past, we've learnt to play the game out here in France. We're gamblers. Death plays against us with loaded dice. The stake for which we play is life with honour; if we lose, we still have our honour.

I should be ashamed for you to see some of the things which I've written you. They're not worthy. They don't represent me in my highest moments, I'm not the kind of person that I've painted myself. I'm not really. I volunteer for a piece of dirty work and take my chances with the best of them. If anything goes wrong I don't whine; I take the consequences. In your case I've volunteered for your sake to be silent; so I'll keep my bargain, and take my fifty-fifty chance just as cheerfully as I would in any row up front. But – let me make just one excuse, my dear – you came upon me so suddenly; you awakened such longings; your very presence spoke so loudly of a future which, perhaps, I may not share; you offered all that I had once hoped for before I put hope behind me. Don't you understand? I'm greedy through starving; I cried out before I was aware. Somewhere in the Bible the story is told of how the people in a city brought their sick and laid them in the streets, so that even the shadow of St. Peter passing by might rest on some of them and heal them. Your presence to me was like St. Peter's shadow to those sick men; it healed me, but it made me long for more than the shadow. The thought that you would walk through other cities where I could not follow, filled me with emptiness.

That is ended. Because I love you I will be happy; not to be happy would be treachery. I have never lost the greatness of the vision of what we are doing; now it should take on a new glamour and knightliness. This outwardly squalid tedium of filling sand-bags to build gun-pits, being strafed and gassed, watching for long hours in crumbling trenches, takes on a complexion of romance. You stand beside me and watch me. All of a sudden the war has become an Arthurian legend in which you and I are the leading characters. I used to say, "I am doing it for her." You have become the symbol of all the goodness for which I fight. Did you ever hear of Gaston de Foix? He was the gayest soldier of the Italian renaissance – a slip of a lad with a soul of laughter, eyes like strong wine and hair that was honey-coloured. Every defeat was changed into victory by his presence. When the walls of a beleaguered city were so slippery with blood that nobody could climb them, he stripped off his hose and shoes, in a spirit of deviltry bound his right arm behind him, fastened his lady's kerchief about his left and, grasping his sword, led the storming party to success.

He took these long chances that he might add glory to the name of his lady. I have no kerchief to bind about my arm, but your letter lies near my heart and goes with me everywhere as a talisman. That you do not know this does not matter; it is in keeping with a war that is anonymous. Like Moses, we climb a mountain and return no more; no man knows the place where we are buried. We kill men whom we never see and are killed by unseen men in return. Our very letters give no indication of where we are. Our address is monotonously the same and monotonously characterless – B.E.F., France. We are allowed to write nothing of what we are doing; we can only record what is happening in our hearts. It's splendid that the world should demand so complete a giving of ourselves. Gaston de Foix rode back from his enterprises to cities garlanded to do him honour. Poets made songs about him, which were sung in moonlit gardens. Feasts were given in praise, at which he sat with the lady of his heart. She wore the token which he had stained with his blood; she knew that it was her love that had given him the courage.

But we – there are too many heroes today for any to be noticed. We have becomes nations of heroes. To be brave is the work-a-day standard; not to be brave is the dastardly exception. We slip back from the trenches into the murk of London unremarked. We come on leave-trains, as walking-cases and on stretchers. There are so many of us that few people notice if some do not return at all. It was easy to be a Gaston de Foix, watched by all Italy while you played the gallant with your lady's token on your arm; but to go out into the night of unknowing, to achieve the improbable and call it ordinary, to live un-thanked, die in a crowd and yet be thankful for your chance – that kind of fearlessness beats all records. It's the kind of fearlessness that is possessed by the humblest of our Tommies. I love them, these chaps of mine. I should find heaven horribly unhomelike if there wasn't any khaki.

The other night I went up to relieve a man in a Forward Observation Post – an O.P., as we call it. It was a dirty kind of hole in the battered trench, with mud a foot deep which stuck to your boots like glue. Just as he was leaving, he threw me a copy of *Scribner's* Magazine, all tattered and splotched. It was an old copy, as most of our magazines are. "There's a poem in there," he said. "It's called, 'To the Beloved of One Dead.' It's true. Read it."

After I had settled myself in the kennel in the side of the trench and had scooped out a hole in the wall for a candle, I started turning the pages. This is what I came across:

> *The sunlight shall not easily seem fair*
> *To you again,*
> *Knowing the hand which once amid your hair*
> *Did stray so maddeningly*
> *Now listlessly*
> *Is beaten into mire by the summer rain.*

I think I said, "Good Lord!" My telephonist looked up and asked, "What did you say, sir?" "Nothing," I answered. The poem was by a woman; I forgot to notice her name. It's too late now. But how did she, living in America, manage to express something which she had not seen, concerning which we who have seen it are inarticulate? Whenever I see a hand thrust out above the mud 'I have just such thoughts; " The hand which once amid your hair did stray so maddeningly." There used to be elbows and arms in the Somme which we knelt on to lift ourselves out of the water, when we were up forward observing. I used to thank the dead men beneath my breath for the charity which their bodies still showed us.

There's a middle verse to this poem, which has slipped my memory. But the third verse ran somewhat as follows:

He died amid the thunders of great war;
His glory cries
Even now across the lands; perhaps his star
Shall shine for ever
But for you, never
His Wild, white body and his thirsting eyes.

In that last line I see the picture of my own soul calling to yours. It's intolerable. 'His wild, white body and his thirsting eyes!' It is better that you should not know. Besides, when the glory has been achieved, the wild, white body should be forgotten. Thank God, you have not learnt to touch me or feel the need of me. – A few pleasant friendly letters, some of which even now may be destroyed; a handful of happy recollections of hours of companionship snatched in Paris; a little kindness in your heart, but no regret – I hope that for you there will be no more than that. "He was a nice fellow," you'll say; that will be all. But to be haunted by those other thoughts! That would be damnable. Besides, it isn't the body that counts; it's this something which, while it cries out for you, refuses to let me turn back, but drives me on and on – to what?

IX

IT has come – your third letter. I had to wait longer for it than you intended, – for we have been on the road for more than a week marching, pulling in for a new attack. It is to be the greatest, so they say, of the entire War; I never saw so many troops in one area or such a heavy concentration of guns. All the way, for the past eight days, I have seen nothing but ammunition-lorries, battalions, batteries, caterpillars, all moving in the one direction. It speaks volumes for the Army organization that, in so vast a movement of such masses, they know absolutely at any moment at what point on the road any unit can be found.

We started with our line of march all routed – the exact number of miles to be covered each day, the villages at which we were to halt, the watering-places, the points for drawing courage – everything ordered and thought out. We moved like clockwork: there were no hitches, no breakdowns.

Some of our poor old horses died; they had been standing in

the mud all the winter. It was pitiful to see them limping along, putting their last ounce of strength into dragging the guns. Their drivers, who had grown fond of them, were still more pitiful when they had to part with them. It's extraordinary how eager men are to give their love; they give it to their officers, to one another, to dumb animals. You wouldn't think that men whose business it is to kill could love so much.

It has been splendid getting into clean country again. The signs of spring were everywhere. We saw women ploughing and little children doing men's work. Only the very old and very young are left; one realized how much France has suffered.

It was tremendous fun after the same old trenches to be going to a new place. The new trenches are just as bad as the ones that we have left – only they're different and that makes for excitement. When you've been on a front for a certain time, you get to know every inch of it. It bores you to death; you get horribly fed up. You don't a bit mind going to something worse if only you can get a sense of novelty.

We stopped in all kinds of villages by the way and slept in anything – from chateaux to stables. We were so weary that where we slept didn't matter much, so long as we got a shakedown and something to eat for breakfast. Each morning we rose at four and usually didn't pull in to our horse-lines till the light was failing. Then the guns had to be parked, the parades carried out, the pickets posted, the guards mounted, and the billets of the men inspected; so it was usually ten before one rolled into his sleeping-sack. By eight o'clock next morning the camp was empty – tidy as if we had never been there; by nightfall other campfires would be burning, surrounded by another crowd of transients. Hymn writers may well compare the instability of life with the passage of an army marching forward.

Where we are now, we have not had time to build any dug-outs; all our work is being put into the gun-pits. When they are done, the men's quarters come next, and last of all the officers'. I have some old ground-sheets spread across a trench in the bottom of which I have unrolled my sleeping-sack. It's oddly like a grave, especially in the dark when your hands touch the cold damp walls. So long as it doesn't rain I'm pretty comfy and haven't much to complain about. One gets used to anything. It's queer to reflect that there's scarcely a beggar in any city who isn't better housed. One can get accustomed to anything when the standards of privation are arbitrary.

This new offensive fills us with excitement. We know that it's going to be costly. The shelling has already increased, proving that the Hun has his own ideas of what is planned. It makes one wonder how many of the masses which have marched in for the attack will march out. Will they die haphazard, blindly, at random – or does some one know already the names of those who will lie silent before the month is out? One would like to ask God questions.

There's an extraordinary suspense and secrecy in the air – an under-current of strained intensity. The men feel it; you see that by the way they work. They spare no labour in making their gun-pits as shellproof as possible. You hear them telling one another, "It's going to be a hell of a strafe when it starts."

The rumour is that behind us the cavalry are mustering, so it looks like Armageddon with a vengeance.

It was here that your letter found me, just after I had groped my way into my sack. I heard some one tramping about on the edge of the trench above me: then my batman asking, "Are you awake, sir? There's a letter for you." I told him to fling it down. When I had played my flashlight on it and had seen your handwriting, you may imagine me hunting feverishly for a match. When I found the box it was damp – so there was I with no way to light my candle, keeping you waiting as though I had no manners. It was just like that, as though you had rung the bell and I was leaving you standing on the door-step. It seemed horribly discourteous after your long and dangerous journey, all the way from J——— to where I am.

Jack Holt sleeps in the same trench, with his feet against my head. I roused him with my swearing. Yes, I am not an angel; there are occasions when my vocabulary grows exceedingly stormy. Jack Holt is a funny old thing in some respects: he sleeps with his head inside a kind of bag. I suppose his wife made him promise to wear it – she must have knitted it for him. That's the only way I can account for the stoicism with which he puts up with our chaff and persists in wearing it. When he speaks with it on, his voice sounds muffled as though he had a hot potato in his mouth. As I continued to swear, he tried to say something. At last I listened. "Use your flash-lamp, old boy. I often use a flash-lamp to read my wife's letters." My flash-lamp was weak; the battery was running out. If it isn't improper, I ask you to picture me as I sat up in my narrow grave, trying to spell out your racing characters by an illumination of about two glow-worm power. Very often I mistook your words; once I thought I had found a sudden tenderness which, on a second puzzling over, vanished. It made my heart stand still for a moment. I realized then what a gaiety would fill my world if I had the assurance that you loved me.

You do not, for you write to me – how often? Once a month, perhaps. Your replies are dragged from you by my many effusions. Unless you forbade my correspondence, you have no option but to reply. I have given you no grounds for doing that as yet; in all that I have written I have been prudent – only the quantity gives you reason to suspect. The quantity constitutes a kind of blackmail; for ten of my pages you can scarcely send less than one in return. But you must know that I care for you. However formal and merely friendly I try to make my letters, there must have been stray shades of meaning in which I have betrayed myself. And then there are the presents which you have received from Paris with no donor's name attached – orders which I have sent back from the Front. They come to you anonymously, chocolates, books, cigarettes. Bad taste on my part to do it! I own that – but I must feel that I am with you, somehow. The books might easily give me away, for many of them were mentioned while we were together. The ones I have sent are those that you said you had not read.

You refer to one of them casually in your letter – *The Journal of Marie Baskirtseff.*' You say that you've come across a copy at J———, and remembering our conversation have read it. Perhaps you're giving me my chance to confess.

Yes, and I remember that conversation, I had called for you on a winter's evening. I had been delayed at the last minute, and then I couldn't find a taxi. As I crossed the Place de l'Étoile I was a quarter of an hour late. How immaterial that would have seemed had I been going to meet any other person! But there were to be so few quarters of an hour that we could share. When I coveted all your life, to throw fifteen minutes away was like squandering a fortune. I found you waiting for me; you were alone, as you always were. I never saw you with another man. From the first time we met, you gave me a strange consciousness that, so long as we could be together, you were reserving yourself for me only. Perhaps it was only because I was on leave. At any rate it was kind of you and made me happy.

I can see you now, snuggled up in your furs, your tranquil hands folded above your muff, and your gloves trailing. Your eyes – how grey they were! Grey as stars when a mist drives across them. They were watching for me; the moment I entered they met mine with a quiet laughter.

I have never tried to describe your face – I scarcely know how. It is a vivid face, small in the forehead and sloping from the temples to a chin that is exquisitely pointed. It makes me think of those long – dead women who, loving life delicately, were made to pose for a renunciation that was not theirs in the sacred masterpieces of Renaissance painters. Always about you there was an atmosphere of mystery, of patience, of beauty half-awakened. I had the continual feeling while I was with you that at any moment you might vanish. I have had the same sensation of unreality in a June garden, when rosebuds were unfolding, and the dew was still glistening on their petals: a poignant certainty that they could not last – their spirituality was too ecstatic. Spirituality is a repellent word; but there is a spirituality of the body. It was the spirituality of the earthly part of you that made me walk beside you with bated breath.

Your eyes are wide, with an Oriental sadness, which is contradicted by the gaiety of your mouth. But it is the brows above your eyes that sum up your character. They are mere pencilled bows, like the arched wings of a bird. That night they were coming towards me; now they seem poised, uncertain, as though a strong wind were forcing them back. What would I not give for one hour with you? Just one more hour.

You rose and held out your hand. We slipped into the night. Where should we go? I think neither of us cared. Had you said, "To the end of the world and for ever, "I should have been made madly happy. We tried the Crillon, but it looked dull, like a swimming pool out of which the water had been emptied. Then we determined to experiment; Do you recall where our experiment landed us – in the Café de Paris, a place where we never ought to have been together? We didn't realize that at first – not until the sparrows of the night commenced to drift in in pairs. When they had perched on the gold-plush cushions, and had begun to preen themselves before the many mirrors, we became aware.

"I'm awfully sorry," I said. "I'm afraid I oughtn't–" – You smiled your amusement. "Life's interesting. So long as you're not worried, I'm –" And you shrugged your shoulders.

I loved you for your frank acceptance of the situation, but most of all for your way of letting me off so lightly. It was so honest – so fearless. So we sat on, ignoring our surroundings, and it was then that we drifted into our conversation about Marie Baskirtseff. You hadn't read her. Did you know Bastien-Lepage's *Joan of Arc* in the Metropolitan Gallery? Well, he was the man with whom she had been in love – probably the only one. I told you of her life, like gold thread woven on black satin – a streak of glory in a cloud of darkness. How she had had two overpowering yearnings – to be famous and to be madly loved. How she wrote down the cruel truths about herself from her earliest childhood – her infatuations, experiments, disillusionments, despairs. How she was trained for the opera and her voice failed her. How she painted the one great picture we had seen in the Luxembourg, and then learnt that she was dying of consumption. When it was too late, love, which she had increasingly coveted, came to her. She met Bastien-Lepage, who was also dying and, when he was too weak to come to her, had had herself carried to his studio. Fame eluded her just as love had done; her journal was not published till after she was dead.

"I wonder if love always comes too late," you questioned. I looked away from you. The temptation was too strong to tell you. You must have known then. "We had better be going," that was all I said; but as I helped you on with your furs I dared not watch you. Before my inner vision the passion of life was marching in procession. I saw what might have been – what might be yet. I had never known love or passion till then. It seemed so easy, so right to seize it while life lasted. It need not have been too late if — but I could not do it — could not speak the words which would destroy your rest. If you had ever noticed me, you would soon forget. What right had a man who was going into battle to leave a woman who might have to weep for him? So I left your question still a question. Perhaps for us, as for Marie Baskirtseff, love had arrived too late. We passed out from the warmth and glare, and parted in the night of unknowing.

All this I remembered as I lay in my narrow trench with your letter tucked beneath my pillow. Every now and then I would get my flashlight out to re-read a passage. I kept hoping I might discover some hidden meaning — some underlying tenderness that your words had suppressed. The guns opened up; the night firing had commenced, shaking the walls of my narrow dwelling. I pictured the Hun carrying-party above which our shrapnel had begun to burst. They would throw away their burdens and scatter. We were sweeping and searching; we must surely kill some. Why should we kill them? We had never even seen these men. Life was ruthless. It withheld love till it was too late. It put weapons of slaughter into our hands, when all we desired was to live ourselves. It gave us glimpses, only glimpses, of the things we had desired, and then passed us on into another world.

I don't know how long I had lain reflecting or whether I had drowsed; the next thing I knew was that the walls had fallen in on me and I was struggling to push back the load from my chest. I couldn't have been buried very deeply, for

I soon smelt the air; it was foul with bursting shells. I made my way to where Jack Holt had been lying and started tearing back the earth. In the darkness one felt horribly impotent to help. Several gunners came running with spades from a gun-pit. They were the detachment that had been doing the night-firing, and had seen the shell that had buried us. I took a spade and commenced digging desperately. We soon uncovered his face – or, rather, that extraordinary bag that his wife had made for him. When he felt the air, he soon recovered and only complained of bruises.

Our flash must have been seen by the enemy or else he had guessed who was doing the damage. He was bringing a concentrated fire to bear upon our battery, doing his best to knock us out; There was no sense in staying near the position so long as that lasted, so We ran from gun-pit to gun-pit, telling the men to clear to the flanks. There were three of them wounded, but none of them seriously; so we didn't come off so badly. The rest of the night was fairly exciting, spent in putting out flaming ammunition.

When morning came, I and my batman set to work exhuming my sleeping-sack. We recovered both it and your letter. I am now residing in another trench. This acquiring of new apartments is very simple in a land where one pays no rent.

But your letter! By the light of day I have read and re-read it. Somehow at each new perusal it seems more friendly. I wonder why that is? Probably because when first it arrived I expected too much; I had written in my mind so often the kind of letter

I would like to receive from you. I was looking for that letter in your pages rather than reading the one you had sent. Because I didn't find it, I sank into the abyss of despair. Then, little by little, I began to listen to you, and finding that you meant to be kind and friendly I cheered up.

Little Gaston still holds your affections evidently. And he isn't so old – looking now, you tell me, and his eyes are becoming increasingly heavenly. But it's his little hands that go to your heart – they're so lonely. You speak of the way they clutch you and hold on so tightly, as if he were afraid of facing life by himself. Poor little chap! He hasn't got much chance – a Boche baby with his French mother dead. War seems glorious when you view it by armies, but its details are tragic. There are so many people to whom it does not give a chance. I'm here to make it still more tragic; your business is to try to mend the things that I have broken. I like to think of our friendship as that – a partnership between duty and mercy.

Ah, and I forgot – you don't approve of Marie Baskirtseff; you think that she was cold and selfish, and brought most of her troubles on herself. I understand – the greyness of your eyes explains a lot. The French have a saying which divides the world into two classes – those who love and those who allow themselves to be loved. Marie Baskirtseff belonged to the latter, while you, with your mothering grey eyes, want to gather all the loneliness of the world into your breast. You would not like her – and I am glad. There are times when I think of you profanely, as if you were the mother of God Himself.

X

WHY don't you write to me? I almost wish that we had never met. Life is unbearable without you. I don't want you to love me; all I ask is a sign that you remember. Surely it is impossible that you should live so in the thoughts of one whom you yourself forget. When my letters come do you smile – smile in a pitying way that would hurt me if I saw it? If you don't care for me, why don't you tell me? But perhaps you are telling me – by your silence. Or perhaps you are only blind. Do you say, "What a nuisance? There's another letter from that troublesome man. Oh well, he's in the trenches. Some day when I'm not so tired I'll be kind." And yet I – I am only happy when writing my soul to you on paper.

You can't guess with what suspense I watch for you each night and how I treasure your handwriting when I get it. All the while I'm ashamed that I should feel this way – that I should allow you to revive this clinging to life. From the first I have never felt that I should come back. Does it seem too much to ask that one girl should only pretend to be a little fond of me? It wouldn't cost you much – half an hour a week of yourself in writing, and I should be happy. You wouldn't need to commit yourself in any way; you would only have to say you were my friend.

I'm afraid of growing bitter up here in the loneliness – rebellious that, with all that life has withheld, it should have forbidden you to me as well. My mind is filled with pictures of what we might have done if –

But I seem to be blaming you – to be accusing you of cruelty. I'm not. I understand. For the first time you have lost yourself in service; you're so absorbed in your work, so compassionate, so weary, so eager to give more than you have, that there's no room for other emotions. Unconsciously you ignore me. If you think of me at all, you attribute to me your own fine altruism. To speak of love at such a time would be like turning from Christ to the embraces of a man – from the divine to the merely earthly.

Oh loose me! Seesth thou not my bridegroom's face
That draws me to Him? For His feet my kiss, My hair, my tears He
craves today – and oh,
What words can tell what other day and place
Shall see me clasp those blood-stained feet of His!
He needs me, calls me, loves me: let me go.

It is almost as though you spoke. They are words that Rossetti put into the mouth of a woman who turned her head when pleasure beckoned, and caught a glimpse of Christ for the first time. She was passing out of a hot Eastern street to a banquet, when she was halted by the divine face. Her lover could not understand. He did not want to understand. He questioned her:

> *Why wilt thou cast the roses from thine hair?*
> *Nay, be thou all a rose – wreath, lips and cheek.*
> *Nay not this house – that banquet house we seek.*
> *See how they kiss and enter. Come thou there.*
> *This delicate day of love we two will share,*
> *Till at our ear love's whispering night shall speak.*

But to this and all his arguments, following Christ with her gaze, she murmurs.

> *He needs me, calls me, loves me: let me go.*

In what you are doing I don't think you are conscious of any religion; if you were, it would spoil it. Nevertheless, what you are doing is religious. You are experiencing the 'expulsive power of a new emotion' – the emotion of a dedicated sympathy; it pushes all personal affection beyond your horizon. You think – if you think at all – that I also am like that; that I, too, have made my heart a monastery. I had. But now, because of you, I crave once more – only once more 'the touch of live hands.' If I could tell you! I wonder. Would you understand?

XI

I AM becoming an old man. It's extraordinary how quickly war ages one. There are boys of twenty in my battery who look forty: their faces are hollow and their cheeks lined. In my mind I am getting like that. This trick of talking to myself on paper is the habit of a person very aged. Well, what does it matter, so long as it makes life happier?

There are times when I almost persuade myself that I have sent you these letters. The world of the heart is an unreal place at best, full of false hopes, false fears and unreasonable charities. I remember how, when I was a boy at school, I used to long for the night to come. By day I was bullied and controlled and miserable, but at night, when the dormitory was in darkness, I used to own my soul and wander where I chose. I created the most extraordinary world for myself, making up with imagination for the disillusionment of reality. By day I was a wretched little white-faced creature, the youngest boy in the school, who crept through the corridors in perpetual fear of chastisement. But at night I was brave – quite a King Arthur kind of person, who rode to the rescue of great ladies and challenged all the world. In my little white bed, one of a row of twenty, I would strive to keep myself awake, lest the hours which were my own should slip from me, and I should open my eyes to find that I was again in the bondage of daylight. Here in the trenches I have fallen back on that old trick of childhood. I have to meet you somehow.

No, my dearest, I am not a coward; I am quite ready to die. I should even feel oddly ashamed if I survived when so many a better man is dead. Don't think I'm a coward. But since we have met I have become most poignantly eager to live more fully. It seems as though I never knew what to do with life till now – now that it is too late. Nothing that I could have done with fifty years of living would have been as splendid as one week of what I am at present doing, but it does not include you. In a vain attempt to make you a part of my world I lie awake imagining half the night. What a foolish heart I have! If you have ever loved, you will understand.

At present much of our time is spent in building gun-pits in advanced positions, too near for safety to the front-line. I am in charge of the construction of one of these just now. The Huns seem to have become aware of us. Doubtless, one of their aeroplanes has observed us. We never know at what moment the shelling will commence. They sweep and search, groping for us with shrapnel. There's scarcely a day that I don't lose some of my men. This is the second advanced position that I have built, and there's a third, still further forward, to be built yet. It will have to be done at night.

The other day a splinter of shell caught me on the head. It made a fairly deep scalp-wound, but didn't seem serious. I suppose I ought to have been more careful. The brigade M.O. wanted to send me out, but there's too much to be done and I don't want to miss the big offensive. I'm staying on at my job, but the wound has become poisoned. My top-knot is wrapped in bandages and I look tragic. The truth is, we're short of officers with all we have to do, and to go out just now would leave other people overworked.

I've mentioned Jack Holt several times. I found that he was worrying because his wife was expecting little Jack. He was up forward the other day at the O.P. when a telegram arrived at the battery telling him to return the England at once – her condition had become critical. We were wondering how we could work his leave when Stephen came into the dug-out. I think I've mentioned Stephen to you; he's the chap who never gets any letters and never seems to expect them. He's a fine big fellow – the kind people love at once; but oddly he seems to have left nobody behind who cares. He was smiling as he entered. "My leaves coming through for Blighty," he said. "They've just told me at Headquarters." Then Jack must have my leave-warrant. There's really no reason I should want to go back to England." He insisted, but he made the proviso that Jack should not be told because, if he knew, he would certainly refuse to take it. Stephen volunteered to take his shift at the O.P. and go forward at once to relieve him. If you could picture where we are and what the contrast between

84

this and Blighty means to us, you would know what that piece of unselfishness meant. Two hours later Jack reported back. We'd hurried up the leave-warrant and he started back for life, hot water and clean-sheeted beds. He couldn't imagine why he was being sent back to Blighty out of his turn; for fear he should worry, we didn't tell him. We're waiting tiptoe now to hear whether everything has gone all right. We're like a lot of old women, we young men at the officers' mess. We've already selected alternative names for the baby according to its sex. We consider that it's in some way ours – a battery baby. In the event of it's being a boy, we've agreed that it must be called Stephen – there's no feminine equivalent for Stephen, unless it's Stephenetta. It would be rather cruel to call a baby-girl that.

You may think it odd that we should take such interest in a brother officer's exceedingly domestic affairs. It isn't really odd – it's envy. We all wish that we also had a child. By calling it a battery baby, we seem to acquire a share in its paternity. Things become very honest and real out here. We reckon up our lost chances. We know why we were born: from Nature's point of view simply and solely to reproduce some one like, but a little better than ourselves. There's an incompleteness about "going West" when you leave no one behind you. But that doesn't bear talking about.

As I write, some one has set the gramophone going. His selection is appropriate, but I wish he'd quicken the time. A thin music-hall voice has commenced to whine, "All that I want is somebody to love me, and to love me well – very well."

Vulgar songs can quite often express our deepest emotions

very truly. Bill Lane has suddenly ceased strafing; an absurdly seraphic look has descended upon him. He's thinking of the girl he is planning to marry. Our major is leaning forward with his head between his hands, scowling as he always does when he thinks of his girl. And I – I'm remembering Paris and the greyness of your eyes and the smallness of your hands, and – yes, thank God, I'm thinking of you doing your duty. The picture of you at J—— is always with me, and the danger, and your own comfort in order that you may make the world a little better. I think you'd like Stephen; he's like that too.

XII

A CURIOUS thing has happened; so curious that I should not have imagined it possible in my wildest dreams. Yesterday I received your photograph. You do not believe me? But I did. I can prove it to you. It is a picture taken in a French courtyard. Climbing from the right-hand corner to the left is a staircase. Standing on the stairs there are one, two, three – let me count – six American Red Cross girls. At the bottom there is a made chef kind of person, who does not command my interest. He has a silky, bird's-nest sort of beard, as all chefs ought to have. To his right, in the courtyard itself, there is a French officer; and to his right a charming little matron; then two more officers and a doorway, in which are standing two American nurses, one of whom is yourself. You are all in white – even your shoes are white – and a white veil blows back across your shoulders. Now are you persuaded that the photograph is really one of you?

How did I receive it? Who sent it? I am no wiser than you.

All I know is that you didn't. On the back there is writing, simply stating that it is from a Sister in an American unit now in France, who heard me speak when I was in America.

Isn't that luck for me? You would never have sent me your picture. I should never have dared to ask for it. Yet, in spite of your reticence and mine, it has come to me, and I carry it with me in my tunic pocket.

An accident! Yes, but so many accidents have happened to me and you. I begin to be superstitious – superstitiously hopeful. We first met in America, the night before you sailed. Without design we meet again in Paris. We spent the whole of my Paris-leave together, never planning anything, but always just chancing to be together. We part with no pledge given – only the memory of happiness we have shared. Then, after weeks and weeks of loneliness, in which I had begun to despair, I receive your picture from an anonymous hand. It looks as though divine providence were chaperoning us. It's made me feel madly, riotously glad. It's as though you belonged to me – as though all of this that I write were not rank impertinence, but proper and allowed. I can believe at this moment that your heart quickens and grows tender when I think of you.

Surely, you, too must have your dreams. Is it too absurd to think that I walk through them? You are young, as I am; though you're in the midst of death and sorrow, the reality of things ended cannot absorb you. It must make you the more hungry for the happier future. It makes me want to live life so much more fully – to grasp everything that is kind and beautiful in my two hands and hug it to me. If ever this inferno ends, what a use I will make of the days that are left! Fancy what it will mean to wake up one morning and know that there are whole years of mornings before you, all yours with no threat of sudden extinction. Just at present I can scarcely believe such a day possible. It would not be wise to look forward to it; the looking forward would make me careful. In this game one cannot afford to be careful of himself. But, my dear –

I've been looking again at your picture. How exquisite you are – how cool and distant! I glance down at my clothes, stained with the corruption of the trenches – what am I to you? What can I ever be to you? How coarse and strong and brutal I am when contrasted with your fitness! This work which I am engaged on does not make one's externals splendid, whatever improvements it may make in one's soul. We do not look heroic. We look pestiferous, and verminous, and very weary. Never again will any of us be young men. I do not understand women. Perhaps they will make allowances for what has happened; it has happened and is happening to us for them. Do they care? Perhaps I do you all an injustice, and you do care immensely.

I should like to think that there are women in the world who will be very compassionate to us when war is ended. The Frenchwomen are like that already. In their hospitals they call a wounded man 'Mon petit,' and take him in their arms and hold his head against their breasts. That is what we need most when our strength is spent – women who are so shameless in their pity that they will mother us. We daren't ask it for ourselves, we shall never tell you. Yet here, in the trenches, we dream about such tenderness. We've been killing men today – we shall be killing men tomorrow – yet our hearts are the hearts of romantic boys, dreaming all the while about girls like you. I sometimes wonder what God does with those of us who die unsatisfied. I think He must place us in the arms of the gentlest of His woman-angels. What we crave most of all is rest and the mercifulness of a woman who cares.

Weak and foolish! I have read what I have written – yet it is the weakness and foolishness that make our strength. If we did not build a barricade with our bodies, your body would be wounded. They call the maimed in France 'Les Glorieux.'"These disfigured soldiers on returning home, become the most honoured men in their villages. Their scars are not repulsive to the women – they are the brands of honour. Though the brand has been stamped upon their faces, the scars cause no disgust in the onlookers. These scourgings of war make their victims "glorious," because they have been borne for their nation. There are four girls offering to marry every maimed soldier in France for every girl who is accepted.

Ah, how these French shame us with their superior humanity! We have called them immoral, lax, sentimental – so many foolish words in the past. I wish to God that we Anglo-Saxons shared some of the vices that produce their virtues. We pretend to be so strong, so self-sufficient, so indifferent to affection. How sick I am of my own pose of spurious manliness! What I want is to feel your arms about me and your lips against my eyes, whispering, 'Mon petit.' Why should I be ashamed to tell you? Why should you be ashamed to do it? I understand the gratitude of Jesus for the woman who pitied Him so abandonedly that she wiped His feet with the hairs of her head. She was trying to say to Him just what these French girls say to their wounded. 'Mon petit,' pressing the weary heads against their breasts.

Wild, wild talk, my little American! I fear you would not understand it.

XIII

The show is commencing in earnest. Every day we have casualties. It's this third gun position that's doing it – the one that we're building just behind our own front-line. We only work on it at night when the moon is down or under cloud. But the Huns have got suspicious; they must have heard sounds or caught glimpses of us by the light of their flares. At any rate, one of their snipers makes us his speciality and there's a machine gun which rakes us at regular intervals. It's really rather exhilarating dodging the beggars, but I hate to see my chaps go down. In the darkness it's so difficult to tell whether anyone has been hurt. The men pass the whispered question from gun-put to gun-pit, "You all right? Is Bob there? Is any one missing?" Then the word comes down to me, "Coxon doesn't answer, sir. He must have got it." So off I go with a couple of gunners to grope through the darkness for the missing man. When we find him, he may be dead or unconscious. The stretcher has to be fetched and men told off

92

to carry him out. We're muddied to the eyes and drenched, but we work feverishly till the first blush of morning, then we sneak away with the shadows.

Poor Stephen got killed up there the other night. You might remember Stephen, the officer in my battery who never had any letters. I shall always remember him by that. There we were, when mail had been brought up by runners, all so happy for the moment, bending above our affections. Stephen just went on working; he had nobody who cared. It was the sniper who got him with a bullet through the head. It happened the night before Jack Holt got returned from Blighty, so in a way Stephen gave up his life lending Jack his leave-warrant.

How soon one forgets his pals at the Front! We have no time for remembering. Any display of grief is a waste of energy. Whether man or officer, it makes no difference, the body is wrapped up in a blanket, unwashed and with the blood of the wound dry upon it. Nothing is removed except letters from the pockets. The boots and leggings are left on, just as he fell. When the mess-cart comes up with the rations at night, the body is sent down in it to the waggon-lines. Next day, in a desolate field that has been consecrated, there is a funeral. A hole is dug of just sufficient size to take the dead man; there's no sense in making graves too comfortable when there's so much digging to be done. Certain of the gunners – officers and men from the neighbouring batteries – are sent down to form an escort. There's always strong competition for this detail, as it means that one can get a bath before returning to the guns. A funeral means very little more than this to any of us – a chance to feel clean for twenty-four hours. The ceremony itself lasts only five minutes; then we turn away and mount our horses. "I may be the next," is what we are all thinking. Well, I hope my pals get a good wash, with plenty of hot water, as a reward for attending my obsequies.

Jack Holt's baby was born while he was in England. Great excitement in our mess! It turned out to be a little girl and we've all agreed, in the light of what has happened, that she must be called Stephenetta. We're blackmailing the mother to curse her child with this name by presenting a christening bowl with Stephenetta engraved upon it. If the infant isn't called that, of course the bowl will have to be returned.

We all wish that Jack could get a respite from fighting, now that he's become a father. There's only one way in which this can be worked – by his applying for a transfer to another branch of service. If he did this, he'd have to live in England for a time while he went through a new course of training. We don't want the father of Stephenetta killed just yet, so our major has persuaded him to put in for the Flying Corps. If the application goes through, he'll be at least made certain of six more months of living.

The dear old chap has brought back all kinds of snapshots of his baby. She's attired in everything – from long clothes to Nature's garment. He's really quite absurd about her, discovering all kinds of intelligence in her always-the-same countenance. In one he insists that she's the image of himself; in another like her mother; in another she has the eyes of his brother, who was killed with the cavalry on the Somme. Well, we've got to keep him from being killed, anyhow.

Since he has come back and I've seen how life can clutch at a man through a woman's love and children, I'm glad that I did not tell you. I don't want to feel bound up with life too much; I see every day what a tremendous lot this new reason for living is costing Jack. Those two, in England, are never out of his thoughts. He's hungry to be with them. I've forgotten which of the Greek philosophers it was who said, "Love no man too much; for he who loves too much lays up sorrow for himself." It's terribly true; love exacts its full price with anxiety for every moment of exaltation. And yet I would gladly have Jack's anxieties, if I could also have his certainties. To go out solitarily, as Stephen went, is lonely work.

A selfish argument! He's left no one to cry. He did his job and asked no one to share the burden of his sacrifice. This being loved and being remembered that the heart so passionately yearns for is nothing but a pathetic survival of the last bit of selfishness. There will be no one either to remember or forget when a hundred years are gone. For those who have done their duty and died, surely God has His recompense. To men who have been so unjust to themselves in their wholesale abnegation, God can hardly fail to be generous.

Though it were for the last time, I should so much like to hear from you. That, too, is selfishness.

XIV

I HAVE been given my job for the big show. We expect that when the attack starts we shall be able to advance to a great depth. If our infantry find things easy, they will soon get out of range of our artillery, so we are building a road for our guns right up to the front-line. On the day of the show this road will have to be carried on across No Man's Land, over the Hun front-line and as far as his support-trenches. Most of this work will be done under his barrage, and I have been detailed to the job. I shall have a hundred men under me. They'll all be volunteers, as they'll only have what's known as a fifty-fifty chance of coming out alive. They'll have to be stout fellows; our orders are that our wounded are to be left where they drop. The road has to go through at all costs. We've already begun the first part of it. We work only at night, just as we did on the forward gun-pits. It depends on the moon at what hour we start; but it's usually about midnight. There's no smoking allowed, no talking above a whisper. The moment the Hun flare shoots up, we lie flat, hugging the ground. Then up we jump and commence filling shell holes, putting in planks in the worst places and building bridges across the trenches. I think the enemy has guessed what we're about, for he keeps a whizz-bang battery eternally sweeping and searching for us; every night, from his point of view, he has some luck. This perpetual number is damnable and splendid. Our men's courage leaves me breathless. It is only the undiscussed nobility of their purpose that keeps them going. It isn't orders; it isn't pay; it isn't the hope of decorations. It doesn't matter who or what our men were in civilian life, they all show the same capacity for sacrifice when in danger. Some of them were public-school men; some served behind counters; some were day-labourers. We have several who have been in gaol; they're every bit as good as the others. War has taught me, as nothing else could have done, how to love and respect my brother-man. I feel humbled in the presence of the patient unconscious pluck of these fellows. I wonder whether I, in their shoes, could be as good under the same circumstances. They usually carry out twice as much they're ordered. They're rarely sullen. They're almost always cheery and helpful.

But the long strain is telling. We wish with all our hearts that the offensive would commence. It's far easier to go through hell for twenty-four hours than to carry on in the mud filling sand-bags, building bridges, working feverishly under the cover of darkness, digging and digging till every bone in one's body is aching. We officers are all hard at spade-work, we do it for the sake of example. It's no good urging your men to dig harder if you're sitting down with a cigarette in your mouth yourself.

I spoke about the suspense getting on one's nerves. We've had a curious case of it. Poor old Stephen had a dream before he died. He thought that he was in a wood and came across a little white cross in a tangled underbush. On stooping down he read, 'Sacred to the Memory of Jack Holt.' You will remember Stephen was killed while Jack was still in Blighty. On Jack's return he said to me, "I already knew that Stephen was dead." Then he told me exactly the same dream, only when he went down to examine the cross he read the one word – Stephen. One dream has been fulfilled, but the other – I hate to record it. I feel as if the mere recording of it might help to make the prophecy come true. We're all of us doing our best to keep Jack out of danger; when some piece of especially dirty work falls to his share, we usually manage to get under the major to let one of us take it. Jack can't make it out, and we don't tell him. He thinks that why ticklish jobs don't come his way is because the major distrusts him. I hope this transfer to the Flying Corps goes through before the show starts in earnest.

I never hear from you at all nowadays. Directly the letters arrived at the guns my heart used to start thumping: I was so sure that there would be one from you. Nothing like that happens now. I know at last for certain that I am nothing and you have forgotten me. And yet there was a time when – or do I deceive myself? You could not help writing to me if you had ever cared. You are breaking the news to me slowly by your silence. Perhaps that is the kinder way to do it.

Oh, my dear, if you knew what you mean to me in this

small handful of days that are left. I know that love in one who is not loved, must always seem absurd. I know that I ought to smile and bow in a gallant sort of fashion, excusing myself for having been so mistaken as to have troubled you with my affections. But the man who used to love like that loved lightly; they had scores of years before them to seek their love elsewhere. I love you as a man loves only once, and I may have but a few hours. You do not know this, so why do I complain? Judging from anything that I have said or written to you, you must think me the merest trifler. Together in Paris we just verged on the mildest flirtation; then we parted. Nothing of my doing or saying has indicated that there is any reason why you should take me more seriously. There is no reason that I have acted in the way I have. My resentment is not for you, but for myself, because, in the disguising of my real emotions I have succeeded too well.

I am writing this by a guttering candle pressed into the wall of my dug-out. It's nearly midnight. I can hear the click of picks and shovels as the sergeant-major distributes them among my men. In a few minutes he'll be saluting in the doorway. "Working-party ready, sir. All present and correct." Then I shall go out to where the shadow-group are waiting for me and we shall start forward to the front-line. The first part of the way is between tiers of gun-pits, where eighteen-pounders spit fire every few seconds. Then we come to a field full of wire-entanglements, where we have to tread warily. At last we strike a road, about three inches deep in mud. It is thronged by night with every kind of vehicle; by day it is dead as the Sahara

Desert. Down this we plod, splashed by passing lorries, till we reach an ammunition dump and a small trench-tramway. This tram-way we follow to where the Hun is shooting up his flares, then we sneak across the open, just behind the front-line, to the point which our road has reached at present. There we shall work like moles. Orders will be passed along in whispers. The wounded will be carried back in silence. The path for the guns will be pushed into No Man's Land. At the first streak of dawn we shall creep back exhausted. I can hear the men joking outside. They're laying odds as to who will get a Blighty tonight. One man seems pretty sure he's going to get it; he prefers it in his left arm, he says, because that will leave his right O.K. to place about the waist of his girl. Unconquerable fellows!

There's the sergeant major. "Working-party all present and correct, sir." I nod. I'm coming. I've been a beast, my dear, in some of the things that I've written. Some day, when you're in love, you'll understand and pardon. I hope he'll be a decent fellow. Because I've talked with you I feel happier; you are nearer to me now. We shall do good work tonight.

XV

IT is the last day; tomorrow the show commences. My men are all chosen. In the choosing of them what trumps they proved themselves! First the gunners of the brigade were called together; there were to be fifty of them. Then the colonel and I went down to the waggon-lines and asked for the same number of volunteers from the drivers. In both cases the colonel made them same speech to them. They were needed to follow up the infantry and to build the road in advance of the guns. He explained to them fully their chances of wounds and death: that the moment the attack commenced the enemy would clap down a barrage on No Man's Land to prevent reinforcements from coming up; that they would have to work in the very heart of this barrage, and that if they were wounded they would have to lie where they fell. Then he asked who would offer himself for the job. Both at the guns and the waggon-lines every man stepped out. Our difficulty was to select the candidates for death without giving offence to the others. I have two officers under me and four N.C.O.'s. I have divided my party up into four groups: two to fill in shell-holes, one to cut wire, and one to bridge the Hun trenches. Most of our materials for this work are already hidden in the craters out in No Man's Land.

You've no idea how exhilarated we all feel. I suppose people at home imagine that when a destruction such as this is pending we are wrought up and stern. Not a bit of it. During the wearisome preparations we were, but now that we're in for it up to the neck we're wildly happy. I can't explain our psychology – I suppose it is that danger makes a challenge to the spirit. By this time tomorrow we shall certainly some of us be dead, but we shall also have achieved sudden glory. Out in the sunshine you can hear singing everywhere. The servants are polishing up their officer's leather and buttons, so that when the show starts they may look spick and span. My chap, without a word from me, has got out my swaggerest breeches and tunic. It's the same with the men. If we die, we shall die swells. We've done everything that can be done now; there's nothing that has not been thought of ahead. We have chosen new waggon-lines, nearer to the guns, so that the horses may be brought up as soon as they are wanted. My brigade will fire for four hours tomorrow, then hook in and move forward to where the Huns are living now. As soon as this position is vacated by the guns, it will become the new waggon-lines. As the advance rolls forward, each battery will hook in and move ahead in rotation, the one which is the last becoming the first. Goodness knows where we shall sleep tomorrow night. The bringing up of the guns will probably be expensive both in horses and men. The enemy will be sure to shell our road under the direction of his balloons and aeroplanes. It' a big game, and the games allures us. It isn't often given to men to have their courage so tested; no one knows what chances he may have for heroism. I think it's that, the consciousness that we are helping to save lives and to make history, that elates us.

As I write, some officers from other batteries have dropped into our mess. They've got a pack of cards out and are playing poker. Everybody's laughing and merry. We're not at all what people at home would imagine us.

The spirit of risk has got into my blood. I can think of you quietly, contentedly now – not selfishly, as I have been doing. How grateful I am that we met. What a jolly companion you were to me. I haven't lost you yet. If I come through tomorrow safely, I've almost a mind to write you a real love-letter. I can picture you reading it, if I were to send it. Those straight brows of yours would draw together. The more impassioned I was, the more puzzled you'd become. It would all be so sudden after my carefully proper letters – letters which, however proper, you have not answered. I'll drop you another line presently – a quite polite one, saying what a good time we're having and how all the mud has vanished; a letter like all the others I have sent, giving you the impression that war is fun. Ah, well, so it is – fun punctuated by long intervals of blood.

Some time ago I mentioned that I'd been wounded in the head. I still wear my bandages, and am so vain that I wouldn't have you see me for the world. The poison has broken out all over my body and I look a leper. A good many of us are like that; I suppose we get it from eating insufficient vegetables and living in damp dug-outs. I'm glad I didn't let them M.O. send me back to hospital; I'll go and get attended to when the attack is ended. Or, perhaps, I will – one never knows one's luck.

I wonder what you're doing. I picture you in your children's hospital, going from cot to cot and playing the mother to the motherless. I keep on writing to the old address, believing that you are still there.

Jack has asked me to take his hand at poker. He wants to do what I'm doing – write to the girl whom he loves best in the world. I'll perhaps add more later.

❧

It's ten o'clock at night. Every one is sleeping. I tried to, but couldn't. I've written to all my people – they may be the last letters they will get. I've written one to you as well. Now, having ceased writing, I'm just thinking aloud. I've told my servant, if anything happens to me, to burn all the papers he finds in my kit-bag. So you'll never know, my dear; I shall slip out of your life and leave you untroubled. Wasn't it wise of me to do as I have done? You've not had the inconvenience of refusing me. I've not had the pain of being turned down. I've kept the illusion that you are mine to the end.

At midnight my servant is supposed to rouse me. He's a good fellow and is sure to have something hot ready for me. I shall put on my revolver and Sam Browne, then away with my men to the front. I've chosen a trench just behind the infantry's jumping-off point: I believe it will be out of the Hun barrage. We shall hide there till about half an hour after the show has started. Then I shall go forward with the other officers and runners to reconnoitre the road through the Hun country. I feel the way I used to at Oxford the night before Eights Week commenced – eager and nervous and wishing it were ended. I used to row stroke then. I'm to do something of the same kind tomorrow – I've to set the pace and keep the heart in the chaps. I wonder how many tomorrows life has for me.

Bill Lane is talking in his sleep. He thinks he's surrounded by Germans and he's refusing to surrender. It's hard on him that he couldn't get married before this racket. If he were married, it would be still harder on the girl. I suppose there are just heaps of men tonight who are thinking just such thoughts.

Why was it that you couldn't care for me? Lately I've often asked the question. It's so evident that you do not care. Queer that I should have gone through life and never have attracted love! There are so many women in the world that there ought to have been one – there's hardly a driver or a gunner in the battery, to judge by their letters, who hasn't got a sweetheart somewhere. There are some who have many. You see, I learn all their intimate affairs from censoring their letters. I'm not regretting. Don't think that. To have been allowed to feel towards you as I have has been quite reward enough. It was wonderful that the most tragic thing in life should have come to me just as life was ended. There's always the chance that I may live to come back. I'm not sure that I should care to come back if you did not want me. there would be a fitting completeness about dying now. And then –

Shall I tell you? Ever since war started I have hoped to die in France. So many others have died that it would not seem fair if I came back. This is the one chance I shall ever have of laying down my life for other people. I don't want to miss it. I have missed you and so many things that I don't want to miss that. The body hampers one; for my part. I could easily do without it.

I can hear my servant stirring. Ah, he's just looked in and was surprised to see me dressed! He's a good chap and has a real affection for me. He's been – how shall I put it? – almost motherly to me. Very often today he's said to me, "I hope you'll come through it all right, sir. I couldn't bring myself to look after another officer."

He's splitting wood now, so as to light a fire and boil some cocoa for me. Now he's getting out my shaving-kit, so that I may go forward with an appearance that will do him credit. He wants to know if I'm going to write much longer. I've told him that I'm not.

You're sleeping. You heart has been always sleeping when I have bent across it. That does not make me love you less. Perhaps, if all life lay before us, I should have tried to arouse it. We met too late for that.

I shall think of you as I lie in hiding with my hundred men waiting for zero hour, when the thunder of guns will open up. Good night, my little girl, whom I did not try to awaken.

XVI

HOW many days is it since I last spoke to you? All that has happened in the interval seems a tremendous nightmare. I'm sitting in a smashed Hun gun-pit, seven miles away from where I was before the offensive started. We use this gun-pit as our observing post. It's on a ridge, and from here one can gaze for miles across a plain girdled with towns. From the chimneys in the towns plumes of smoke are drifting, but in the plain, where thousands of men are in hiding, nothing stirs. Every acre of it, as far as the eye can reach, is enemy country. Far away balloons gaze down on us. Falling precipitously from the ridge into the plain is a slope which was once thickly wooded. The branches are stripped clean of leaves by shrapnel, and the underbush is putrescent with human bodies. Everything is dead.

For myself I am a sight to mock at. My swaggerest tunic and breeches are swagger no longer. For nearly a fortnight I've not had them off; they're caked with mud. I need shaving. My head is on fire with the old wound and the bandages are dirty. To complete the portrait, I got a slight wound in my shoulder which has stiffened. You wouldn't want to walk through Paris with me now. The men who are with me look still more disreputable. They live in a dug-out which must always have been verminous, and is ten times worse now. The hot spring sunshine on the corpses has started a plague of flies. Directly you set foot in a dug-out you can hear the buzzing of their wings as they rise up to settle on you. Here in the open it's not quite so bad, but if one doesn't eat quickly his food becomes black with them. I sleep in the open, in the gun-pit beneath the battered gun, and take my chances of shell-fire. I can't stand the smell of decay which one gets underground.

We have to be careful how we move about; the least sign of our presence brings down a barrage. And yet, for all the rottenness of our situation, we enjoy ourselves in a terrific fashion. We've driven the devils back seven miles, which is not so bad.

The show was glorious. I have never experienced anything like it. The last time I wrote to you was just before I went forward. Well it was about 2:30am when we dropped into the trench in which we were to hide. It was bitterly cold. The men joked in whispers, keeping their spirits up, making bets with one another as to who would get wounded first. They didn't have to wait very long to find out, for some battery commenced to fire pre-matures, which got us in the back. Towards four o'clock everything grew silent – literally silent as death. All night in thick flakes the snow had been falling. Even that stopped now.

The whole world seemed to listen with bated breath. Slowly the darkness began to melt; the faint dawn crept throughout the horizon. It was a sign.

We consulted our watches, counting first the minutes, then the seconds. There was a gasp; we had reached zero hour. As if the heavens had fallen, hell broke loose with a crash. Behind us, like hounds in monstrous kennels, the guns commenced barking in a deafening chorus. Where our shrapnel was bursting, snakes of fire darted across the Hun trenches. A little ahead of us, with a triumphant shouting, our infantry leapt up; we could see them, silhouetted against the pale background of the sky, pouring over No Man's Land. The Hun took a good five minutes to reply, then down came his barrage like the stamping heel of one who was tormented. Our second wave of infantry rose up and disappeared into the smoke of the carnage. The air flapped in tatters. Our ears were deafened with explosions. On the other side of No Man's Land flames spurted where our chaps were bombing defences and dug-outs. One had to keep himself from imagining. Of a sudden something even more terrific happened. The Hun started to send over liquid fire. His shells burst about thirty feet above the ground and poured down flames as if from buckets.

I waited for half an hour, then, leaving my men in charge of one another, I took the other one with me together with four N. C. O.'s and four runners. We carried Union Jacks on poles to mark the direction, and pegs, with tapes attached, to stake out the road afterwards.

From now on I have no very clear recollections, only general impressions. I remember the wild laughter of the chaps who accompanied me, and the curiously winged sense I had, as if I had already cast aside my body. For a moment we halted on the top of our trenches. No Man's Land boiled and bubbled like rocks over which a tumultuous sea was breaking. It was strewn with the dead and dying. There were men with broken spines and legs, clawing their way on hands and knees through the mud to get back to safety. Every thirty feet or so shells were detonating, throwing up a spray of death. How human reason could survive was a marvel. It seems unreal to me – a horror which I have read about.

In every curtain of fire there is a rent, which can be found if you keep your head and look for it – a place where the fire of two enemy batteries has not joined up and has left a gap. I found one; in single file we commenced our advance. In old shell-holes to right and left of us dead men were lying, men who had been caught by the liquid fire, and had flung themselves into these pools to put the flames out. The pools were all cochineal in colour as if with blood, but really with the explosives. Wounded chaps called to us to help them or simple gazed at us desperately. We passed them – we had no time to help – and came to the Hun wire entanglements. Here we planted the first Union Jack, and told off an N.C.O. and a runner to tape the road back.

The Hun front-line was a sight which I shall never forget. I suppose it must have been five feet broad and at least six in depth. It was a river of blood, choked to the brim with dead and dying Germans. They lay there silent, waxen, with eyes wide but dulled. Many of them were pounded into pulp. They had all been alive that morning.

I shall sicken you if I go on. No words can convey the picture; it was horribly inhuman, pitiful and glorious. You won't understand the last adjective. No one could who had not been there. It was glorious because it was so immense.

Four times we planted our flags, and each time sent an N.C.O. with runners back. At the farthest point we met the first batch of prisoners. They were so foul that you could smell them at a hundred yards. They were about fifty of them; their sole escort was a Tommy with a bloody bandage round his head and a rifle cocked, whom they carried shoulder high on a stretcher. Far away, through the haze of battle, we could see our infantry still advancing, following behind our bursting shells. Then we turned back to get our men to work. I found them in the trench where I had left them, and was about to lead them in through the barrage when our colonel came up. "You'd better wait," he said. "Surely you're not going to take them in through that?" I told him that I was. Before he could give me orders to the contrary a shell got him. I have since heard that he is dead.

My chaps were splendid. There wasn't one who didn't work his heart out. Very soon the Huns commenced gassing, and we had to wear our masks. Its no joke to wield a spade in a mask, but these chaps never stopped. Every now and then one would topple over. Sometimes he proved to be gassed and sometimes wounded. If wounded, we bound him and up and left him. If gassed, we led him out of the barrage to recover; when he was better he invariably came back. Their pluck was superhuman.

Presently I got sick of having to leave my wounded men where they fell, so I started on a search of the Hun dug-outs. Most of the former tenants were dead, but every now and then I would find some in hiding. I routed a gang of them out and turned them into stretcher-bearers.

It was about midday when our first battery came up and got into action just behind us. It hadn't been there long when an enemy plane swooped down and turned its machine gun on them. The gunners who weren't carry ammunition, or firing, had to stand with rifles and try to pick off the pilot. What happened to them afterwards I don't know, for the building of the road carried us beyond them. From now on, brigade after brigade of field guns commenced to overtake us. They followed us so closely that it was difficult to keep ahead. The moment they had reached us they unhooked and got into action.

One of the officers under me had been killed by this time and very many of the men. In the afternoon about two hundred more reported and we made better progress. But towards evening the rain descended and our progress ended. The battle-field became a sea of mud, and the road which we had built was cut up too badly for any more traffic.

We were weary and drenched to the bone when we started back in search of our battery. Our enthusiasm was exhausted. Through the gathering shadows burying-parties were groping, picking up the dead. At the guns nothing had been built but the gun-pits; they were little more than soggy platforms. Rain was trickling with a malicious constancy in every direction. My batman had found what was left of a dug-out, of which he had dispossessed several corpses. There he had spread my sleeping-sack. I was too tired to eat or undress; having taken my boots off and drunk a tot of rum I fell sound asleep till morning.

Between the days that followed I cannot distinguish. They were full of adventures and physical misery. It snowed and rained; we were never dry. We were always pushing our guns a little farther up. We lived always in the mud. What we ate didn't seem to matter. It was for the most part iron rations – bully beef and hard track. So much for our miseries.

Our adventures were made up of going forward to the ridge to observe. They were real adventures. One never knew where our infantry were for two days together. We had got away from trench warfare; for the moment we were engaged in a moving battle, which consisted in taking pot-shots from haystacks and shell-holes. The enemy had been driven down into the plain; it was the business of the gunners to keep him there. We got chances at many targets. The plain was dotted with towns in which the enemy troops were concentrated. Along sunken roads and between hedges his battalions were continually marching. All day, from sunrise to sunset, we observers pushed our telephone lines forward, that we might send back word of latest developments.

I think the most wonderful sight I saw was our cavalry riding down to capture a certain town. I was hidden in a haystack within ten feet of them as they passed, and could see the whole progress of their charge. This is what I saw. When they reached the plain, they bent low in their saddles and set off at a gallop. They came to a village from which Huns came out carrying the white flag before them. Our chaps halted, parleyed, swung round on their haunches, and came tearing back, lying low along their horses' necks. I learnt afterwards what the Huns had said: "We have two whizz-bang batteries trained on you and any quantity of machine guns. You had better surrender." It was true. As our men commenced hurriedly to retire, the Huns opened up. I saw horses cut clean in half, and men crashing from their saddles in all directions. When they again passed my haystack there was not more than half of them left. They seemed demented; death pounded behind them.

But even more dramatic was the scene I witnessed two evenings ago. I was forward as liaison officer. Suddenly, as the sun was setting the whole Hun front-line started to move back. They looked like a swarm of ants as they rushed eastwards. I phoned the news to my Division, and was recalled to help guide the batteries up. What a night I had! Everywhere horses were foundering. The mud was like glue; it held them down when they fell. By dawn only one of our batteries was in action, and our infantry were due to attack. Again I went forward, only to find that the infantry were out of range of the guns. As I came into a certain town, the Huns were engaged in street fighting.

Our battery is in that town now, and the line has again moved forward. The wire in front of the support trenches has been put up behind us. If battle goes against us, we can't pull out. We're what's known as a 'sacrifice battery.' We hold the Hun until our guns are knocked out. This would all have sounded terrible to me before war started, but now, in a strange way, I rejoice in the terror of it. It's splendid to find that you can gaze into the eyes of death and remain undaunted.

I think of you, as I shall think of you to the end, if the end comes. I do not want you less. I want you more perhaps, only not so selfishly. I realize that death does not finish all things. Love lives on. There are other worlds – there must be so many other worlds – in which I shall surely meet you if I miss you in this one. That I, so poor and human and puny, should be capable of this largeness of spirit, gives me confidence that God's scheme for us must be greater than we have guessed. He cannot be smaller than the souls He has created. You may not need me in this existence. We may have met too late to be much to each other. But I cannot think love is wasted. Those men whom I saw piled high in trenches so loved their ideal that they could die for it. There is something god-like in such self-abnegation. 'God so loved the world that He gave His only begotten Son;' these men so loved the world that they gave themselves. Though the ideal for which they die may be mistaken, whether they be English, French, or Germans, they seem somehow to strive up towards God's level. To do that is religion. I am almost jealous of them – which must seem strange after my ghastly description of them.

And yet there is always you, you, you, to lure me back from death. You with your grey eyes and your intense atmosphere of rest – you with your unconscious womanliness. I should like to know that when I am dead you would take me in your arms and give me the kiss which, while I lived, were not allowed. That wish is mere sentiment. What good would your lips do me when mine were silent?

XVII

WHERE we are now we are compelled to lead a topsy-turvy sort of an existence. We have pulled into an orchard among a pile of ruins, in full sight of the Hun. We have knocked holes in a wall, through which we have pushed the muzzles of our guns; for the rest, we dare not build any overhead cover, but have simply strung up camouflage netting. By day we dare not move about for fear we should be spotted. Enemy planes are continually passing over; one man seen walking might give away our position. So we hide in holes in the ground by day and work like fiends by night. There's another reason why we have to lie low: this place is continually under bombardment. We are here to fire with open sights if the enemy breaks through; meanwhile we fire only in attacks and when an S.O.S. has been sent up. It's pretty difficult for the Hun to pick up our flash when all the batteries behind us are kicking up a dust. What a life! Who would have dreamt in 1913 that we should be taking part in such an adventure?

We're all dog-tired, but full of fight. Our infantry haven't been relieved since the first day of the offensive. They're gaunt and haggard and determined; they're bone weary and full of passionate contempt for the Hun. When they aren't fighting, they're sleeping.

The dug-outs in which we live are many steps underground. The Hun left them in a filthy condition; by degrees we're getting them cleaner. We scarcely dare to light fires: the smoke would make our presence known. We have very little water – only bottled stuff that the enemy left. We can't trust the wells: they're usually poisoned either by accident or intent. There was one we used for a day or so, until we dragged up a part of a dead man on the bucket. That taught us a lesson.

It seems always night now. We don't venture out of our subterranean darkness till evening has gathered; with the first hint of dawn we again vanish underground. Through the telephone we are in touch with the open world, where spring is waking. It's difficult to imagine that somewhere flowers are blowing. What wouldn't I give for one more spring of freedom with all the sweet and fragrant smells? How we shall value the little beauties of life if we manage to survive this valiant hell!

It's about six o'clock in the afternoon. In about two hours we shall climb out and start to work. Behind us, leading over the ridge, there is a broad white road, down which at night the ammunition is brought to us. It is carried on pack-horses. If we used the limbers, they would be heard by the enemy; then again, if a limber were hit or ditched, it would hold up the traffic. Just at present we're building pits to take our shells and trying to get some cover over them. The important thing is not to make tracks: they would be recorded on enemy aeroplane photographs.

After such a long wait, two nights ago I received your last letter. You hadn't quite forgotten me. You hadn't forgotten me at all. You have been ill, but you're better now. You don't tell what was the matter – only that it was a slight septic poisoning contracted through a scratch, when you were doing something for a wounded solider. What was that something? I want to ask so many questions. But you must be better now, or you wouldn't be back on duty.

So they sent you down to Monte Carlo to convalesce! You give a gay picture of the dashing Serbian officers who are recovering from wounds or on leave there. I like that explanation one of them gave you of his gaiety, 'We do not wish to live to be old – only to live while we can.' I suppose if I had acted on that principle I might have won you. I couldn't. I couldn't forget that men were dying and fighting. It was impossible to seize my own legitimate happiness and not to remember. Was this weakness or strength? I don't know. One can't retraverse the past; nothing can change things now. Like that young Serbian, I have no wish to be old – only to live while I can. I had my chance to live while we were in Paris, but I hadn't the heart to take it; I couldn't forget the chaps in the line – my chaps – who had only the chance of death.

I should have liked to have been at Monte Carlo with you. I'm glad you wanted me, but I shouldn't have been happy; I'm happier where I am. You felt that, too – the sense of dissatisfaction that people should dance and be merry while others were placing their bodies between them and tragedy.

The machine-guns have started overhead; it must be getting dark. They sound like an army of typewriters. They're here to protect us in case the enemy breaks through, so that we may be able to fire till the last moment. We have our plans all arranged if this should happen. The guns are to be dragged out to the right flank, so that they can fire point-blank at the enemy. One officer is to be left and three gunners of each gun-detachment; they will keep the guns in action until the range is no more than two hundred yards, then blow the guns up and escape, if they can.

"Ammunition up!" The word has just come through the phone from the sergeant-major's dug-out. That means that the first train of pack-horses has arrived and it's time to commence work. The poor horses suffer terribly. Some of them get caught every night in a barrage on the ridge. The road is littered with dead horses and the corpses of men.

The letters have just been brought in. There's nothing from you; but I didn't expect one, having heard so recently.

XVIII

WE have moved out of our last position and are in a place which is infinitely worse. We are absolutely in the open and can now be seen every time we fire. About four miles away there's a slag-heap from which the Hun can observe us any time he likes. The horizon is dotted with balloons, which gaze straight down on us. All the Hun has to do is to take cross-bearings to our flash; the point where the bearings intersect is our battery-position. Directly we open fire, he starts to shell us, just to let us know that he can knock us out whenever he chooses.

When we moved in here we had no dug-outs – no sort of protection whatsoever, things are not very much better now. We have scrabbed various holes in the side of a bank, dug a trench outside and connected them on the inside with tunnels. But the holes are only proof against splinters; a direct hit gets us every time. In front there's an archway beneath a torn-up rail-road; the enemy keeps it under continual fire. We have to pass through it to get up front and never know whether we'll get through alive. We hold our breath as we approach it; then run for it. The men who made a bad guess in judging their time lie twisted on either side. It's a suicide's game that we're playing now – a reckless game of hide and seek with death.

We always know when we've done the enemy a damage. He at once comes back at us with 8-inch shells; They have what are known as 'instantaneous' fuzes which detonate the shell before it has penetrated the ground and kill everything within a very wide radius. He bombards us all day and gasses us all night; we don't get much rest. If we're not in action, we take cover the moment he starts to work. Very soon our ammunition begins to go up in flames; we have to run out through the barrage to extinguish it. Our gun-pits get hit. Our men get buried. We spend most of our time in digging chaps out. It's horrible when they're dead – men whom you've lived with and loved.

The Hun has started a new trick: he sends bombing planes over to finish us off. The other night a section was pulling out two damaged guns when the droning of a plane was heard. The next minute the earth flew up. Out of thirty men and fourteen horses only one man and horse were left. This is real warfare that we're at now. Everything that went before seems child's play. Those of us who get out alive may think ourselves lucky.

And yet the marvellous thing is that we keep happy. Danger is the most heartening thing in the world. Directly a row starts our spirits rise. We have the gambler's feverish excitement; we may lose everything in the next minute.

Our trip into this place was horrible. We made it at night. We had dragged our guns halfway when the Hun commenced gassing. Infantry supports were coming up. We were caught in a narrow part of the road and jammed. How we got our guns through I don't know. We had to drive over living men in places. An attack was expected. We had to get into action. It was too dark to see what we were doing.

I don't know why I should tell you all this. You'll never read it. But I have to get it outside myself; we never discuss what has happened among ourselves. The details of what we are doing do not bear contemplating, let alone discussing. We want to forget them, and are cursed by remembrances.

Ah, my dearest, this is not what we planned to do with life. We had intended to live it so kindly. There was not one of us who ever hoped to carry weapons in his hands. Were I to find myself in your presence now, I should gaze at you strangely. Everything that you stand for – your womanliness, your beauty, your sincerity – is so remote from my experience. I have become something primeval – not ignoble, but more terrible. Death and horror and decay are around me on every side. One turns up the thin earth from bodies everywhere one treads. I have lived too long amongst such scenes ever to forget. Were we to meet, you would not understand my silence. After witnessing so much pain I feel that I shall never again know merriment.

Yet we carry on quite normally here at the battery. We play cards, set our gramophone going, sing in chorus when the agony is at its worst. Instinct tells us that some of our men have been buried; we put on our masks, stumble through the darkness and begin to dig them out. Directly a hole has been made, one of us creeps in with a flash-light and commences binding up the wounded at once. If they are crushed or shattered, we wrap them in blankets and ease them through the tunnels to the surface. We help to carry them out to the dressing-station through the barrage, then return with our hands still stained with their blood to our meal or our game of cards. Water is scarce; blood we see in plenty. Our whole effort is to prove to ourselves that we are still undaunted. The Hun can rob us of many things; he shall not rob us of our courage – our courage which is not fearlessness but self-respect.

At the back of the ridge, where the old offensive started, poppies are growing. In the torn woods, which slope down to the plain, daffodils are thrusting up their heads. High above the guns the larks are singing. Joy is in the air; it is in our hearts also, in spite of the terror.

I dreamt of you last night. It was the first time that this has happened. We were in a garden full of sunshine and roses. You were leaning on my arm. We must have been married for some time, for there was no strangeness in our being together. We came to an old stone summer-house and sat down. You sank your head against my shoulder, gazing up into my eyes and brushing my lips with your hair. You were intensely mine while the dream lasted; then I awoke to find myself without you. Will it ever happen? Will you ever give yourself to me like that? My heart cries out for you and hears only the silence.

XIX

THIS is the end. It cannot last much longer. More than half our gunners are gone; I am the only officer left. The bombardment has been going on interminably; two of our guns have been knocked out. For a moment there is silence; it looks if the Hun were going to attack.

Jack is dead. A shell struck our mess, wounding him and myself and killing the major. That happened three days ago. Jack stayed on to help me run the battery, but this morning I insisted that he should go out. He had walked about a hundred yards towards freedom, when a shell fell right on top of him. There is something damnably vindictive about all this, after the way we have tried to shield him. Four days ago the transfer came through to the Flying Corps, which would have given him six months in England with the woman and kiddy – whom he loved. He ought to have gone away at once, but he was too much of a sportsman. He knew that we needed him. So Stephen's dream has been fulfilled, and the two white crosses will soon be standing.

I said just now that I was the only officer left at the guns; you'll be wondering what's happened to Bill Lane. He's safe, thank God! Before all this started he got his leave to Blighty; he's probably in Cornwall, or some other suburb of heaven, spending his honeymoon with his girl.

⟡

We've just been hammered again. You never saw such a mess as they're making of us. I've been out helping to extinguish ammunition. Our remaining guns are still in action; if the Hun breaks through we shall be ready for him.

I never saw my men more merry. They're like gods. I almost worship them. How do they contrive to rise above such torment? All about them their pals are lying dead. There's been no time to make them decent; they lie huddled and half buried where they fell. Those of us who live are for the most part wounded.

My leg is crushed and I can scarcely hobble; I shall manage to hang on till the end.

Our wires to brigade are broken; the last of our B.C. party are now out trying to establish communications. The ridge is being pounded so heavily that I doubt their success. For two days an almost constant curtain of fire has shut us off from the living world. No ammunition has been able to get up, no food, no water, no anything. It's the same with the infantry up front. We've ceased firing, and are keeping what ammunition is left to hold the Hun if he breaks through.

I'm going out again for a final inspection. Jove, how my leg hurts when I put my weight on it! I feel tremendously cheery. I can hear my chaps laughing. They're planning what they'll do to the Hun if he comes. Danger is the finest stimulant in the world. We've still got our tails up.

There's nothing more that I can do. There's a row going on up front. We daren't fire for fear we kill our own infantry; we don't know where they are at present. All the lines are still down. I sent two men forward to pick up information. That's probably the last I shall see of them. The rifle fire on our left is intense.

If I come through this, I have made a pledge that I will tell you. The last few months have educated me in taking chances. You may not want me at first; I will make you want me. You shall want me as much as I want you.

Why didn't I tell you while there was time? Was I over-scrupulous? And if I had told you? It's the old, old question; I shall 'go West' with it unanswered. I shall never know now whether you would have loved me, or could have been made to care for me. Perhaps you did care, and were waiting for me to give the sign.

My dearest – But what more is there to be said? The things one says are always inadequate; it's the touch of live hands, of lips pressed to lips that count. I want to hold you and to say nothing. I want –